365¼

A THANKFULNESS PROJECT

DEREK BRADLEY

365 ¼: A THANKFULNESS PROJECT

ISBN: 978-1-4866-2117-0
eBook ISBN: 978-1-4866-2118-7

Word Alive Press
119 De Baets Street Winnipeg, MB R2J 3R9
www.wordalivepress.ca

Cataloguing in Publication information can be obtained from Library and Archives Canada.

Dedication

To my daughter Rosandra—Rosie, RoPo, my girl! Each story in this book is beautiful, just like you! You can do anything. You can be anything. Always believe in yourself! You are enough! May you always know that your daddy is *forever thankful* for the gift of you and "the brothers"! I may not always be physically available when life pushes at you. In those circumstances, read a chapter or two and take comfort in knowing you are not alone. Your daddy, God, and so many others are always right there with you.

—Nose Rub Dad

CONTENTS

Acknowledgements

Thanks to the "sit for a bit" lady for her reminder that life isn't about what you don't have; it's about being thankful for what you do have.

Thanks to my mom, who has always been a true example of thankfulness and unconditional love. You are the best mom ever!

Thank you, Ellen! I could not have completed this project without your guidance!

My special thank you to the incredible women who graciously took a leap of faith and unselfishly gave the gift of their story for the benefit of others.

Introduction

You may be wondering what persuaded me to write this book. The answer is quite simple: I was inspired by an unexpected shift in perspective I was gifted from a homeless woman! I had recently had an unanticipated life experience—and no matter how much I tried, I couldn't seem to pull myself out of the funk it put me in. The more I focused on it, the more I began to become unthankful. That changed when a woman inadvertently taught me how to "sit for a bit."

One cold winter day, I decided to go to the mall for some much-needed retail therapy.

After about an hour of browsing, I realized I had become quite disinterested in that whole endeavor. So I sat down and did something I hadn't done in a long time but totally enjoy doing: people watching.

As I scanned the crowd around me, I began to focus on the individuals and couples who looked the least happy. I thought that would make me happy, and just like with my retail therapy, it did. For a while at least.

At some point, my internal "true voice" recognized that I had "stinking thinking" going on. That voice decided to intervene by taking the short elevator ride from my gut to my heart to my head.

Upon arrival, it gently whispered, "Aren't you tired of the reality you are creating? Don't you realize that misery loves company?"

That gentle nudge of truth helped me make the cerebral course correction so I could start looking for what I call a "gooder." Within seconds, I was redirecting my newfound attention towards people who appeared to be having a much more enjoyable shopping experience. And I realized that it made me feel a whole lot better.

About the same time as my internal epiphany, an overtly overdressed woman sat down directly opposite me. At first I didn't pay her much attention, but I soon discovered that in addition to the excitement of her comfy new seat, she had also found a new interest—me. For long enough to make most people feel a bit uncomfortable, she intensely stared at me like I was her last meal.

Never one to shy away from a good stare-down, I decided to engage in her process to see which one of us would break eye contact first.

When she spoke, I blinked.

"Hi, handsome," she said in a calm and gentle voice. "How is your day going?"

A little taken aback, I replied, "Great, thanks for asking. How is yours?"

And then came the gift.

With the biggest smile on her face, she said, "It's great. I'm homeless and just needed to sit for a bit so I can warm up."

Then as quickly as she arrived, she stood up and casually walked away.

They say when the student is ready, the teacher will appear—and did she ever. Who says their day is great when they know full well that the home they're returning to is the cold winter streets? Who smiles as they walk back into their unfortunate circumstance?

It is said that it's not the bite or wound from a snake (a person, event, or circumstance) that kills you; it's the slow and steady release of the venom (one's focus on misguided thoughts) into your body that takes you out.

The key to surviving and recovering from whatever's consuming you isn't to kill the snake or whatever bit you. The key is to get the proper antidote into your system so you can use its power to help you create the way forward to hope, healing, and breakthrough.

Being thankful is one such powerful antidote.

The truth, whether we like it or not, is that growth often comes in many forms, and more often than not those unwanted circumstances are our best teachers. But only if we allow them to be.

As the COVID-19 experience of 2020 has taught us, we all get to experience the good, the bad, and the ugly from time to time. No one is exempt. Fair or not, it's simply the reality of human experience.

However, when life gets us down, instead of giving up and giving in, creating more of our own personal prisons of brokenness, what if we chose to look for the good in and around us? What if, like the homeless woman who was happy to "sit for a bit," we chose to be thankful in all things… instead of blaming the government, our parents, or whatever our own personal sacrificial lamb? Would we be better off? Would our mental health improve? Would we find the thankful part of ourselves again? Could it be that one of the keys to manifesting true happiness in our lives has been in our control this whole time?

I needed to know the answers to all those questions! So instead of leaving them unanswered, I took the unexpected "thankfulness intervention" from that homeless woman and embarked on a one year, 365¼-day thankfulness journey with twenty-five fearless, brave, strong, intelligent, caring, and giving women.

I hope that as you read through their stories, truths, and thankfulness revelations, you will yourself in some way discover thankful moments of your own.

Be blessed. Be well. Be thankful!

Chapter One
You Are Enough

As I waited for my fashionably late friend to arrive at Clementine's, one of the best breakfast places in Winnipeg, it suddenly dawned on me that this was the first step into my 365¼ Thankfulness Project.

I then realized I was a bit anxious. Nervous even. What was I getting myself into? Given all my personal and professional commitments, when would I even find the time for this project? And why had I reached out to one of the most influential women in Canada to start this journey?

Over the years, I have learned that thoughts aren't thinking. Thinking is a skill. So while I was waiting, I asked myself one question: *Are you thankful?*

That profound and life-changing question led me to wonder if I had been taking life for granted, and if the words coming out of my mouth were simply habitual and empty capsules disguised as thankfulness.

As I sat percolating on all that, it dawned on me that thankfulness isn't an event or an experience; it is a state of mind, a way of life. That revelation of truth was perfectly timed, because as I looked up, I was greeted with Sheila's contagious smile.

"Hey Derek! How are you? Sorry I am so late. Have you ordered yet?"

And in the split second before I responded, I had another Aha! moment. My journey was about to happen because I had chosen to move towards my goal of exploring thankfulness. And because of that, I was now about to listen, learn, and grow from Sheila North—one of *Chatelaine* magazine's top-thirty women of the year, former award-winning journalist, and Grand Chief of Manitoba Keewatinowi Okimakanak.

"Hi Sheila," I replied. "No problem. Have you ever eaten here before?"

"No, I haven't," she responded warmly. "But I think I'm just going to have porridge."

"Are you sure? There are a lot of options."

"Well, what would you recommend?"

"Why don't we order the porridge as well as a few other dishes to share? I suspect we will be here for a while."

"That sounds really good actually. Let's do that."

With decisions made and our breakfast order placed, we dove into the conversation. It was free-flowing, effortless, and she was completely engaging. In fact, the more she spoke, the more I understood why God had gifted me with such a humble and caring person to launch the Thankfulness Project.

Eventually our meals arrived, along with the much-anticipated bowl of porridge. Looking over at Sheila, I noticed that tears had suddenly begun to form in her dark brown eyes. It was obvious that she was struggling with something, but I could also sense that she seemed to be drawing incredible strength from whatever had caused her to become emotional in that moment.

"Are you okay?" I asked.

"Yes, umm, sorry. Thanks for asking. These are good tears. When I saw the porridge, it made me think of my dad. Did you know he passed away recently?"

"No, I didn't. I'm so sorry to hear that, Sheila."

"Thank you. Anyway, one of my fondest memories is the porridge he regularly made for all of us when we were little. He was such a great dad."

"You really light up when you talk about him. Can we talk a little more about your father?"

"Absolutely. I'd like that. My dad was the best. He was the type of guy who would give you the shirt off his back. He cared about people and especially his family. From the time I was small, he taught me to value others and myself. He was the kindest, most selfless, most thankful person I knew. My dad taught me to ignore the negative and let things go, but at the same time to not let people walk all over you. He encouraged me to be thankful in all things, and he made me feel limitless. He always told me I was beautiful both inside and out. Even on my last visit to see him at the hospital, he held my hand, kissed it, and said, 'You have been through so much. I admire you.' And then in Cree he whispered, 'Kihminosin,' which means, 'You look beautiful.' I just always knew he loved me. Yup, my pops was quite the man. In fact, I believe he's the reason I am who I am today, and I am so thankful for that."

Even though Sheila had started our conversation with tears, it was evident that her happiness and joy came from within. Her pops had clearly made a huge impact on her, and I wanted to know more about the man she cherished.

"You have a real thankful presence about you when you're talking about your dad," I said. "I didn't know him, but I can definitely see his teachings reflected in the way you live your life. Can you tell me a little more about those teachings?"

"Dad was always teaching. I learned so much by how he carried himself and how he lived his life. And he always made time for people, no matter who they were. He made a deliberate effort to get to know every person he met; he valued them and always made sure to talk to them as individuals. He was also a giver. If he believed in you, he supported you, and he particularly believed in supporting women. He tried to help them get into leadership roles in a time and environment when it didn't happen that often. That in itself taught me a lot. He definitely led by example."

"What story or memory from growing up stands out for you as a teachable moment?"

"I think I was about six years old when I was woken by a loud knock on our front door. It was late at night, and I didn't really pay much attention to it at first. I knew Dad would answer the door because he always answered the door, no matter what time of the day or night it was. Everybody knew there was a warm meal or cup of tea available to anyone who came by our home; that night, I just assumed it was someone taking him up on the offer. I tried to go back to sleep, but my curiosity got the better of me. For some reason I wanted to know who it was, so I snuck out of my bedroom to sneak a peek."

I laughed. "Is that where your future award-winning skills as a journalist started?"

"I guess so! I remember sticking my head around the corner, and my father saying, 'Sheila, come here, my girl. Come.' So I ran to him and my dad let me stay. When he introduced me to the visitor, a man named Elijah, Elijah asked me if I wanted to sit on his lap. I was excited, so I did. I got to listen to both of them talk about life, politics, and other politicians for most of the night. It's truly a great memory for me."

"When you say Elijah, do you mean Elijah Harper, the former Member of Parliament?"

"Yes! He was out campaigning and decided to stop by to have a cup of tea with his old friend."

Can you imagine, at the age of six, being part of that conversation between Sheila's father and the late great Indigenous leader, politician, father, and family friend Elijah Harper? It would have been easy for her dad to send her back to bed, but his decision to include her in their leadership talk was a teachable moment that may have planted the seed for what was to come in his daughter's life. At the very least, Sheila's dad knew that his words, combined with actions, would sustain and nurture his daughter long after he had moved on to the next life.

"That's very cool, and from my perspective, incredible foresight as well," I said. "I never would have guessed that a breakfast item would have such a great teaching in it. I guess it's fair to say that everybody needs porridge."

"I would agree with that. I would also say that every moment we have with our loved ones is a gift, and we definitely need to be thankful for them."

"Just as I am thankful, and truly honored, that you accepted my invitation to be interviewed."

"You're welcome. Is there anything else you would like to ask?"

I looked at my watch and realized we had been talking for almost two hours, and while I could have listened to Sheila and her stories all day long, I decided to cut to the chase and ask the question I intended to ask every person I interviewed for this project.

"Maybe one final question. Of all the stories you've shared, the up and down moments, the goods and the not-so-goods, what are you most thankful for and how has being thankful helped you throughout your life?"

Sheila didn't even have to stop to think. "I am thankful for my parents and how they raised me. I am thankful for their deep faith in God and how they did their best to be loving, caring, and strong-willed parents. Their commitment to their family shows up every day in our families now; we are indeed blessed in so many ways. My parents taught all of us to care for each other, to stay connected no matter how life turns out, to not expect life to always be easy, and to not take anything or anyone for granted. As for what I'm most thankful for, I would say for my dad's unshakable belief in me, his life that showed me nothing can stop you from achieving your goals when you put the effort in, and his words and his deeds that told me every day, 'You are enough!' As for how thankfulness has helped me. I would say that being grateful has given me the opportunity to learn to think before speaking, especially in difficult situations when you're forced to think on things in a positive light. So being thankful has helped me tremendously."

Just as porridge can give you the strength and nourishment to get through the day, so can a father—or another key person in your life—who teaches you to be thankful and lovingly supports you, encourages you, believes in you, and makes you feel that you *are* enough. Never underestimate the power of thankfulness. It is one of life's remarkable gifts!

Chapter Two
Life Is Love

My friend ordered a Grande Pike with room for cream, like she always did. We've only known each other for a few years, but our friendship is one that I really enjoy because we both challenge each other to think differently. She is spirited, kind, and not the least bit interested in what social norms say she should be. She knows who she is and is not defined by the world. She works daily at meditating on the events and moments that bring joy into her life, seeking the lessons in the challenges. It has taken her years to get there, and periodic reminders and reviews to stay there, but she says she wouldn't have wanted to get where she is any other way.

"You ready, Squeak?"

"I'm a bit nervous, but I'm ready," she says. "Let's do this!"

"Tell me about your childhood experiences. Start with whatever comes to mind."

"I've been thinking about what you might ask me. For the most part I had a good childhood. I never went hungry and was able to participate in sports and other activities. My parents didn't have a lot of money, but we would take a lot of road trips and I knew I was wanted and loved. On the flip side, emotions and feelings were not modeled or discussed in our family. The rules were simple: 'If you don't like or agree with something, too bad! Adults know best, so buck up, shut up, and get over it.' That was really hard as an inquisitive little one. To be totally honest, because of this I spent a good portion of my life completely disconnected from myself, struggling to understand and process my wants, desires, and emotions. Looking back now, I can see that my parents were never taught how to process their own emotions. They simply weren't able to model healthy behaviors they themselves didn't know how to employ."

"How did not talking or learning about your feelings affect you?"

"Not knowing, understanding, or being able to talk about my feelings made me feel powerless. My father was severely physically and mentally abused as a child. While he promised himself he would never hit a child—and he didn't—some of the mental abuse definitely impacted me. Sharing how I felt, expressing anything different than my father's view, resulted in punishment. Privileges were taken away. I was grounded for months at a time and isolated from family and especially friends. I learned that having my own needs met meant I would have to be punished in some way. He was very controlling and the only emotion I ever saw him express was anger. That definitely took the biggest toll on me in high school when I was trying to figure out how I fit in the world."

Sadly, because she never grew up learning to manage her emotions, Squeak said she didn't know how to express herself when she was a child or feel secure in doing so. At school, when pushed, she felt a deep anger at her feelings of powerless.

Rebellion found its way into her toolbox and eventually became her default setting when her hormones required her to deal with emotions aside from anger. Acting out also became her norm, and slowly but surely she found herself wandering aimlessly down unhealthy paths, secretly hoping to find security and some validation that she mattered and was worth caring about.

As you might imagine, that brought its own challenges and rarely worked out as she hoped.

"The harder I pushed, the harder my father pushed back," she explained. "Eventually I felt like a bird locked in a cage. I just wanted to escape my life, so I dropped out of school in grade eleven. I was a bit of a wreck, I suppose. Obviously I was just confused and screaming out for love and guidance. That behavior persisted into adulthood and many of my relationships suffered. I either pushed people away or clung to those who weren't very good for me because I thought love equaled control and pain."

As I sat listening to her, I realized there were many parallels to my own childhood experience. I had left home in my high school years, rebelling, and the only emotion I had learned to share was anger. Squeak didn't know it, but I understood her struggle.

I also knew that although it's not easy, an inside-out transformation is possible with perseverance and purpose.

"That must have been tough," I said. "How did you find your way back?"

"After I dropped out of school, my father decided to stop 'parenting' and told me he didn't care what I did. As soon as I turned eighteen, I was out of the house. Having him back off gave me that little bit of freedom I needed to refocus. After realizing that my talents, intelligence, and abilities would be wasted without an education, I enrolled in school, graduated with honors, got my degree, and did my best to move on. I built a great career and lived independently. Outwardly, I looked happy and successful, but inwardly I was still a bit lost emotionally and found that my coping mechanisms didn't work anymore."

She went on to explain that it took a moment of introspection and a lot of failed relationships for her to realize that her romantic entanglements were suffering the same fate—and she was the common denominator. Unable to fix it, and at a loss for what to do, she decided it was time to talk to a professional counselor. For better or worse, counselling started her on a journey back to becoming herself.

"Learning that I had experienced mental abuse was tough, but it helped me see that to move on I needed to reconcile the pieces of myself that I didn't know existed or that I hadn't felt before," she said. "That was good for me, and something that really helps me now—don't laugh when I tell you this—is my Fluffy moment."

Even though she asked me not to, she began to chuckle and so did I. It was perfect timing for a laugh because, as usual, our conversation had skipped the superficialities in exchange for a more heartfelt experience.

After a few minutes of teasing, we finally settled down and returned to our conversation. With the world's biggest grin on my face, I said, "I can honestly say I have never asked anyone this question, but what is a Fluffy moment?"

"Fluffy was my childhood pet hamster, and my sister had one as well. One day I came home from school and Fluffy was nowhere to be found. When I asked my parents where she was, they said they had given her away. They wouldn't entertain any more of my questions after that. I ran into the yard crying and told myself that no one loved me, that I was garbage and no one cared how I felt. Without even knowing it, I had formed a basis of belief about myself that I used to guide my behaviors in life. I unconsciously sought out people and circumstances that kept on validating those unhealthy thoughts and feelings."

Years later, she was having coffee with one of her girlfriends when they began discussing core issues—and Fluffy came to mind. She shared the story with a laugh, and her insightful friend told her, "Now replay the story back to yourself and assess it with the wisdom you now have."

So she did!

There were a number of reasons her parents could have given that hamster away, and none of them were because she was unworthy. Her friend told her to thank her inner six-year-old for the wisdom, but it wasn't her truth anymore and she could release those old thoughts for good.

Suddenly it dawned on her that her parents' approach may have been harsh at the time, but maybe it reflected the best methods they knew. Maybe, in their own way, they had been trying to protect her. Maybe they had cared about her feelings after all.

She did eventually ask her mother why they had given the hamster away and it turned out that it had been to save her from being killed by the family's second hamster.

"Since that Aha! moment, whenever I find myself having an emotional reaction, or whenever I feel defensive, I try to create some space before I react. I take a breath, observe, evaluate, and ask myself, 'What is the core issue here?' Once you can objectively look at that outdated belief and how it guided your behavior, you can address it. After all these years, I finally found that I'm not powerless after all. I have the power to change how I see things and respond. I think of Fluffy any time I need to create the space to reevaluate a situation using my current wisdom instead of an outdated belief."

Her willingness to change combined with her desire to grow emotionally ultimately caused her to begin a new process of deciding what she wanted in life. She discovered that creating a new life isn't only about making changes but about writing your own story. Who knew a hamster would have had such a positive influence in changing Squeak's life?

"One last question," I said. "Out of all your life experiences, how has being thankful helped you, and what are you most thankful for?"

"Truthfully, that I've had each and every one of those experiences to learn from. My experiences helped me to get exactly where I needed to be when I needed to be there. They have allowed me to find love in everything, if I'm willing to look for it, and I'm grateful for that. I am thankful that I'm able to love myself and love again, and I'm grateful that I found real love. Without healing first, there is no way I would have been able to handle it. Love isn't just a feeling; it's effort, commitment, and employing integrity in everything you do and say. Life is not just about what you want. It's so much more than that. Life is love! Being thankful is all part of that."

Even though the emotional strain from her younger years wasn't easy to confront or work through, her decision to do so has given her new skills, structures, and systems to draw from when unhealthy thoughts try to sneak into her life. Like she said, "Being thankful is all part of that."

Chapter Three
Defining Beauty

The birth of my daughter has been one of the best things to happen to me. I can't explain the feeling except to say that she has a full grip on my heart. I find myself telling her daily that she is beautiful, pretty, gorgeous. Without a doubt, she absolutely is! However, it wasn't until my recent conversation with Jessica that I discovered how important it is to make sure my little girl knows that she is more than her looks.

I first met Jessica while she was working in the food industry. She always seemed to find a way to engage in conversation with people, no matter who they were or what they looked like.

Throughout our weekly encounters, we always seemed to strike up a conversation that reached deeper into who we were as people. Sadly, as life would have it, we lost touch. However, I later came across her profile one evening while aimlessly scrolling through social media. I couldn't believe it! It had been more than eight years.

Immediately my uninvited thoughts began speaking to me. My voice of logic was saying, "Send her a message to say hi." My Poopie Pete voice was saying, "Don't be an idiot! It has been eight years. Move on."

So after about a moment of self-reflection, I came to the conclusion that this wouldn't be the first time I'd taken a risk, nor was it the first time I would potentially end up looking like an idiot. So I parked Poopie Pete's unsubstantiated wisdom and proceeded to send the message.

"Hi Jessica, how are you?" I typed. "I just came across your profile. I'm not sure if you remember me, but about eight years ago I used to frequent the restaurant you managed. You always seemed to find the time to genuinely talk with me. For some reason, those conversations have always stuck with me." I see you have achieved what you said you would. Congratulations! Well done, well done!"

Amazingly, I received a response back within minutes.

"Well hello! Yes, I remember you and thank you. Hope you are doing well also? What have you been up to?"

Often we are presented with the opportunity to take action about something our gut tells us to do, but we don't do it because of fear. More often than not, this causes us to miss out on some of the best chances we are given to learn and grow. However, when we act on opportunities, we often receive a gift that's been waiting for an invite into our lives.

"I'm pretty good thank you!" I wrote back. "I have a busy work and family life which has no signs of slowing down in the near future. I am also writing a book called *A Thankfulness Project*. Feels a bit strange to ask you, but would you be interested in being interviewed for it?"

"Thankfulness! Sounds interesting. I am a writer as well. Send me the info on it and I will get back to you."

To my surprise and delight, a few weeks later, I was capturing her story!

"So tell me something I don't know about Jessica."

"Well, that could be a lot of things," she said, laughing. "I was an international model when I was younger, but you knew that?"

"No. Actually I didn't. All I knew was that you were driven to complete your degree in communications, that animals and the humane society were your passion, and that you were working a gazillion jobs to pay for your schooling. Can we talk a little bit about you and your international modeling experiences? How old were you? How did it happen?"

"For sure. I was super young. A friend and I were hanging out at the mall, just being normal thirteen-year-olds, when a scout from a modeling agency approached me. At first I thought it was a scam, but my mom and I followed up with the talent agency and everything checked out. The next thing I knew, I was flying to Vancouver to attend a modeling convention. That's how I landed my first international modeling contracts in Japan and Korea. Believe it or not, I went by myself. I was basically on my own."

Getting signed to a modeling contract can be a dream come true, but to be a thirteen-year-old girl, working in a foreign country, in an industry that you don't know very well, without any real guidance or support? Let's just say this isn't what I expected to hear.

"That actually seems kind of scary," I said. "Were you scared?"

"At the time, I wasn't afraid. I didn't know what I didn't know. I obviously thought the way you did. I thought it was going to be different… but when I began doing shoots over there, it was tough. Looking back, I realize that it was all kind of crazy! I was put in some situations no young girl should experience on her own."

"Do you mean it was tough because you were on your own or because of what people said to you?"

"Both! When I was in Korea, several of the modeling agents thought it was okay to constantly tell me I was too fat, or I wasn't this or I wasn't that. I was happy with how I looked, but I felt like that wasn't what I signed up for. They were rude and I was so far from home. It was so demoralizing. I tried not to cry, because in all my model training it had been drilled into my head that you don't cry when you model. No matter what. Because if you do, it wrecks your makeup. Then, to make it worse, when I came home there were three types of people at school: ones who liked me for me, ones who liked me because I was modeling, and the ones who called me 'the dumb model.' I didn't really feel like I fit in anywhere. Truthfully, I felt closer to some of the other models I had worked with because they understood what it was like to not fit in. Looking back, it was really hard. I struggled, I really did."

Again, this wasn't what I had expected. She had been blessed with a pleasant appearance, but characterizing a person based on their looks is absolute stupidity. Too often we assume that outer beauty makes life easier for someone, or that it makes you less susceptible to the good, the bad, and the ugly experiences that come in life.

However, that hadn't been true for her.

"Thank you for sharing your experience and how it made you feel," I said. "Maybe it will make some people think before they speak."

"I hope so. Just so you know, it wasn't all bad. I made a lot of lifelong friends from my experiences. It also helped uncover a few internal things for me. It helped me to reflect on what I wanted as a woman. I wasn't going to bury my real self anymore. I'm thankful I did it and that I went through it, but modeling isn't what or who I am. It's just something I have done. I had so much more that I wanted to do… I wanted to be a businesswoman. Just because I looked a certain way didn't mean I couldn't go into business! I decided that if I wanted people to see me for me, I needed to be myself. So I chose to put modeling on hold and go after what I truly wanted."

It was such a great reflection on how her experience had helped her see that her gifts, talents, and character were what truly mattered. I realized that who Jessica was and what she wanted to become in life was hers for the taking.

"These experiences also helped me recognize that I was no longer going to let others define me," she continued. "I'm just like everybody else. I have feelings. I struggle from time to time. Who doesn't? After I came to terms with that, I never looked back. I knew that as long as what I ended up doing was purposeful, I enjoyed it, and it had the potential to make a difference in the world, that was all I needed—whether that was in business, or if I decided to go back to work in modeling."

People often talk about inner beauty, but it's often defined by what others think it should be. I love that Jessica defined it for herself. Today she is a successful businesswoman who leads a dynamic and talented team of professionals who are second to none. She volunteers and recently fulfilled a childhood dream of being a board member for the Humane Society. She's a wife and mother, and she even finds time to venture back into modelling from time to time.

"This is such a good story on perseverance and believing in yourself," I said. "Thank you for today. I'm so glad we have reconnected."

"I'm glad to share. Thank you for asking!"

"My pleasure. When people were mean and said those demoralizing things to you, it hurt you personally. Do you have any advice for others who may be struggling a bit with their self-worth because of demoralizing comments?"

"If I was to pass on one piece of advice, it would be that your worth has to come from within," she said. "I would encourage those struggling with external comments to know themselves and love who they are. Then the rest doesn't matter. Put the work in and learn how to love yourself. Getting to know myself and cognitively knowing that I was a good, smart, and empathetic person gave me the strength to move past negative comments about my appearance."

"That's really good advice. I don't want our interview to end! It's been like old times talking with you!"

"It was therapeutic and great to catch up. We are definitely staying in touch."

"Yes, I would like that. Okay, I have one final question for you: how would you say that being thankful has helped you get to where you are today, and what are you most thankful for?"

"Let me think! I believe being thankful really is a gift to yourself. I'm definitely more fulfilled when I am thankful. As I get older, I recognize that I need to verbalize my gratitude to myself and others. It makes me stronger! I have learned that being thankful helps me to find a way, especially in those times when I feel broken, to be able to say to myself, 'It's just a moment! This too will pass.' You know what? It always does!

"My sister is someone I'm so thankful for. Love her! I didn't tell you this, but I had a really tough pregnancy. The only thing that got me through it was my family and my relationship with her. I couldn't have made it without my family's help. I am completely thankful for them. They helped me close the circle of insanity I was experiencing. It's moments and people like that that I'm thankful for. I am thankful that I've learned that I'm not owed anything and that I recognized early on that you have to work hard for what you want in life. I'm also not perfect, by any means. But then again, who is? Whenever I have a tough day, I tell myself to be thankful. It's so important in keeping the right perspective. The hard work of life will never end, but the craziness of my thoughts will."

We all have moments. We all need support at one time or another. Jessica's teaching is a good reminder that your physical appearance is not who you are and that you should never let it stop you from achieving your goals and dreams. You are so much more than who others perceive you to be!

Chapter Four
Trumped by Love

Several years ago, a friend disclosed to me that she had experienced things no child should ever have to go through. So when I started making my list of possible interviewees for this book, Dorothy immediately came to mind. Not because of what she had disclosed, but because she is one of the kindest and most thankful people I know. I knew that if I reached out to her and she accepted, her work into healing herself could assist many others on their healing journey.

For a while, I didn't make the call, as I was battling whether a story like hers should be shared due to the extreme trauma associated with it. Rather than chasing my undecided thoughts around in my head, I went with my gut feeling and invited her for lunch to discuss the project.

It wasn't more than two cups of coffee into our conversation that she looked at me and said, "Let's do this."

"Are you sure? I know that some of what we may discuss won't be easy to talk about. I completely understand if at any time you may change your mind or not want to continue with our interview."

"Absolutely! I am sure! Sometimes we go through things, bad things, but because of it we may be able to help someone else find hope through our story. I have thought about this a lot, and prayed a lot. I'm ready. Ask away."

At first, I asked all the standard questions I had come to use as ice breakers to support the slow transition into the deeper and more complex components of people's lives that are rarely shared. Eventually, I found myself at a spot in our conversation where I decided to ask about what she had shared with me years ago.

"Remember when you told me that as a little girl you used to bury yourself in the garden to hide from your abuser, so he wouldn't be able to find you?" I asked. "I'm not sure if I said it back then, but I am sorry you went through what you did."

Nodding her head, she looked at me with a strength I have come to admire. "I sure do. As early as I can remember, I never really felt safe. I was very creative in finding places to hide from him. He's no longer alive, and when he died I could finally break that silence. There was also domestic abuse in our home. My dad was mean to my mom, and to all of us, and it was worse when he drank. At school I never really felt like I fit in, and I was always getting into trouble. I know now that all the trouble I got into was a direct result of what happened to me."

Pausing, I found myself at a loss for words. I was truly saddened by what she had shared and began to feel like I didn't want to continue.

"I'm okay," Dorothy said, sensing my reluctance. "It's taken a long time, but I am good. Please, ask away!"

Her response was exactly what I needed. "You are such a strong person," I said, regrouping. "How did you get through it back then?"

"Well, to be honest with you, I struggled for years. But it was the strength and faith in God I witnessed from my mom that has carried me to where I am today. Mom truly was my rock. I always knew that there was something better for me. She told me that daily and I believed her."

"Your mom sounds like she was an amazing person. How old where you when you lost her?"

"Yes, she was! I miss her so much! I was nineteen. She died in a car accident. Her death was so devastating to me. She was my everything, and losing her compounded everything. I went into an unhealthy tailspin of partying for years. I even contemplated taking my own life, but my mother had really instilled in us that this was something we could never do, no matter how bad things seemed. So instead I put myself in harmful situations hoping something would just happen to me."

"What changed?"

"I had a much needed intervention from my mom one day on the way to write a university exam. I had been drinking a lot and was inebriated most of the time. I wanted to stop but couldn't find the strength. It was in my moment of need that my mom spoke to me. I heard her voice as plain as day."

"What did she say?"

"She told me that this isn't what she wanted for me. She told me it was time to straighten out. Hearing her voice really scared me, but I knew I needed to listen to her guidance. After my talk with my mom, I still had to write my exam. I was still a bit inebriated, but I went anyway. When I got there, I just stared at the paper. I was in no shape to write the test and my professor knew it. He motioned for me to come see him."

"What did he say to you?"

"He asked me for my exam and told me to come talk with him in his office at 10:30 a.m. I wasn't sure what to do, so I walked to the student center, grabbed a coffee, and sat down. My hand was shaking so badly that I could barely hold it without spilling. I ran into an old friend there and confided in her everything I was going through. She held my coffee cup for me so I could drink from it. She told me that everything would be okay, and because of that I decided to go meet with him."

When she got to her professor's office, he spoke with her and said, "I've noticed that you are having a tough time. Do you have an alcohol issue?"

Not wanting to go down this path anymore, Dorothy had decided to tell him the truth. "Yes, I have a problem!"

It was then that he offered her an unexpected olive branch. He told her that we all struggle from time to time, and that if she would get help to become sober he would let her come back and write her exam again.

She thanked him, and two weeks later she went back to the university to rewrite her exam.

"After I finished writing it, I sat outside the lecture hall wondering what to do next," Dorothy said. "That is when I first met Lydia. I guess she could see that I was having a difficult time. She walked over to where I was sitting and said, 'I hope you don't mind me saying this, but you look like you could use a friend right now.' She was like my guardian angel. She sat down beside me, put her hand on my arm, and introduced herself. We ended up speaking for a while, and during our conversation I learned that she was a counselor. She gave me her card and told me to come by her office anytime if I wanted to talk further."

Often in life we receive support from some of the most unexpected places. I think everyone would agree that we could use more people like Dorothy's friend, the professor, and Lydia at different times in our lives.

"Did you ever go see her?" I asked.

"Yes, I did. She was so kind and caring. She helped me a lot. She mothered me back to a healthy version of me."

"That's amazing. Interesting how things work! Can you tell me more about how she mothered you back to health?"

"She took me out for dinners and got me another counsellor who helped me work on my trauma. It was months of sessions, talking and crying. I also read a lot of self-help books and did quite a bit of journaling. She helped me to come to terms with my grief from losing the one person I knew had loved me unconditionally, loved me in a way no one else ever would or could. I learned to start caring for myself and believe there was purpose for my life. I am so thankful for her. I've lost touch with Lydia, but she is absolutely one of the reasons I am who I am today."

Not once did Dorothy complain to me about her past during our interview, even though she shared some pretty terrible details. I was astonished by her strength and resilience, but even more fascinated by her ability to truly forgive.

It was also so nice to remember that people like Lydia still do exist. Her unexpected intervention is such a good example of why it's so important to reach out and be kind to one another. You never know what impact your kindness can have on someone else's life.

"This has been a really important teaching for me," I said. "It is once again causing me to self-reflect. So thank you. I do have one last question for you before we go our separate ways: after all that you've been through, can you share how being thankful has played a role in your life? And what would you say you are most thankful for?"

"Being thankful was a value my mom instilled in all of us children, because she always told us things could be worse," she said. "I use my mom's teaching of being thankful to approach each day with a thankful heart. My faith, thankfulness, and the joyful times in my life all have carried me through the tough times. As for what I'm most thankful for, I am thankful for my children and my life. I am thankful for God! I am thankful for faith. I am thankful I had a praying mother, because that's why I am where I am today. I am completely thankful for forgiveness. Letting go was a process, but it helped me to allow love back into my life. I am thankful I got to share my story because it may help someone else. I want readers to know that joy, peace, and love is possible no matter what you have been through. I am thankful for Lydia. I think of her from time to time. She was one of my angels. I also want you to know that I am thankful for you. You helped me find my way back as well. I needed you to know that."

Dorothy definitely has had her fair share of trials and tribulation in her life, but because of her faith and the courageous choice she made to remain thankful in all things her traumatic past is now being trumped by love.

Chapter Five

My Jimmy

As I drove down Stoney Acres Lane, I began to reflect back on my childhood experiences at the Irvine family home. I was good friends with the Irvine boys, but I would be lying if I said that was the only reason I frequented their humble abode.

Their mom, Dora, was a kind, tiny woman full of spunk and with a real zest for life. She valued family—and if you were the type intent on upsetting that, she could easily make you aware that dynamite comes in small packages.

Their dad, Jim, was quick-witted, hard-working, and always managed to keep a happy-go-lucky perspective even when circumstances pressed against him. He treated everyone as a person and didn't give a rat's butt where you ranked in terms of social status. In other words, he accepted you the way you were, whether you were messed-up or wonderful, whichever you thought you were. Simply put, he was an all-around good guy.

Sadly, a few years back Jim unexpectedly passed away before I could thank him for his genuine kindness and the unconditional way he had accepted me and my sometimes unconventional ways.

Thankfully, several years later I was gifted with the opportunity by Dora to say my goodbyes and honor my friend and "her Jimmy."

"Hi Derek, I'm so glad you came," Dora said, inviting me in. "I have so many stories of Jim to share with you today."

"Thanks for the invite and for being willing to participate in my project, Dora! How have you been doing?"

"I'm slowly finding my way. It has been three years now and I have my days, but I have all of our memories to keep me going. How are you, Derek? Can I get you anything? Coffee. Water?"

"Thanks for asking. I'm crazy busy with my family, but I am pretty good. As for something to drink, I'm good for now, Dora. I only have about three hours, so if you're okay with starting the interview, that would be great."

She beamed from ear to ear. "Yes let's start! I have so much to share with you."

"Where would you like to do it?" I asked, and then the inappropriateness of the way I had phrased my question reverberated inside my head. It wasn't how I'd intended it to come out, but thankfully Dora's sense of humor was still alive and well.

"Oh Bradley," she replied, half-chuckling. "That is such a Jim comment. How about we do it right here at the table where he spent most of his time teasing and driving me crazy?"

We both laughed, but it also caused me to unexpectedly choke up. I'm not sure if it was because physically I knew my old friend wouldn't be joining us, but Dora's reply triggered a different thought process in me. Jimmy may not be there in person, but through her reflections and our memories, he definitely would be there in spirit. If I listened carefully, it was only a matter of time before I would hear his legendary laugh again.

"Remember how handy Jim was?" Dora said. "He built our house, for Pete's sake. Remember the cupboards that used to separate the kitchen and the dining area?"

"Actually, now that you mention it, yes I do. Where did they go?"

"That's exactly what I asked when I came home that day. He told me he took them down because they were obstructing our view when we talked to each other at mealtimes. A few weeks later, I ventured out into his shop for something, and lo and behold, there were my cupboards, perfectly mounted and full of all his tools. Apparently he had felt like he needed more storage space. That was my Jimmy!"

I burst out laughing, but the best part was that she did, too. This went on for several hours as she shared story after story about the man she had so loved.

It's fair to say that both of us benefited from our talk, but what touched me more than our belly laughs was the joy that exuded from Dora in her thankful moments. Over the years, I've heard a lot about how the power of a person's focus, whether good or bad, can determine their emotional state… but I didn't expect to witness the truth in action under her current circumstances. It was pretty cool to see how she drew happiness from simply being thankful for the moments she had gotten to spend with Jimmy.

"You keep saying how thankful you are for your time with Jim," I said. "I can feel it. It seems like your reflections about him have helped you work through your loss. Would you agree?"

"Yes, that's exactly right. Those moments keep me going. I am thankful for every day of my forty-seven years with Jim. Thinking on our time together is definitely one of the ways I get through each day. I think about our life together. Sure, we had our moments, but who doesn't? You know, some days I actually feel his presence. Even though he has been gone for nearly three years, he is still with me. He is a part of me. You know, Derek, life is about moments, and he sure left a lot of good ones with me and so many other people."

They say there is power in words, but after talking with Dora I realized there is also exponential power in reflective thankful moments.

She didn't know it, but several months later I too would experience the unexpected passing of a loved one—my own father. That day with her helped me, and continues to help me, get through my personal loss. Because of her sharing, I am now better able to recall my own Jimmy-type moments I had with my father.

"Well, you do light up like a Christmas tree when you talk about Jim," I said. "Forty-seven years is a long time. What initially attracted you to him?"

"I loved his mischievous smile. We started dating when I was fifteen and he was fourteen. Actually, one of Jim's greatest delights was to remind me daily that I was an old woman compared to him. He used to tease me that I had robbed the cradle. He loved to tease. I loved that about him. Even though he could be a royal pain in the butt, I loved it. There was no one like my Jimmy. He had a gift. He could find joy and humor in anything. Literally anything! He loved to string me along and found great pleasure in convincing me that his stories were true. I would always believe him, only to find out weeks later he was just being a smart ass. I miss that. I have my moments, but those memories still bring me happiness. How could I not be thankful for him?"

"I couldn't imagine losing someone after forty-seven years. By today's marital standards, that is forever. If you don't mind me asking, how did you do it? How did you two make it that long?"

"Well, it was not because he was perfect," she said. "He never tried to be. He did stupid things. I did stupid things. People give up too early nowadays. We always understood that it was up to us and no one else. Love is work, but it's worth it. On occasion he would have a few too many, but it wasn't all the time. He'd had a tough upbringing but never complained. He rarely shared that part of his life because he used to say to me, 'What's the point?' He just chose to be better than what he had. He made the most out of what he was given. He was a good man. He would do anything for anybody. He truly did have a heart of gold. Yes, he teased me a lot. Endlessly, actually! It drove me nuts for years, and he knew it, but… you know what I miss the most? His smart aleck comments. Actually, they are some of my best memories.

"You know how great of a husband I had? He would wake up at 4:00 a.m. on his day off, among other things, to make me a cup of coffee and drive me to palliative care so I could volunteer because he knew I was helping people. That is who Jim was. I'm so thankful he was mine. I am going to be seventy this year, and if I could do it all over again, I would. I know I was given a gift. How can I not be thankful?"

As I thought about her last comment, I was struck by the truth of it. Why are we not more thankful? North America has incredible wealth and unbelievable freedoms compared to the rest of the world, but so many people tell you how badly they have it. We have somehow allowed our abundance of material things to distort our perspectives on what being prosperous really means. Dora hadn't. She understood that moments hold the real wealth. Her comment—"How can I not be thankful?"—should be made into a shabby chic sign and hung in every home of our great country.

"This has been really good, Dora," I said. "Thanks for having me over today and sharing your stories with me. I am so glad I came."

"You're welcome here anytime, Derek. I mean that!"

"Thank you, I appreciate that. Before I head out, though, I was wondering if I could ask you a few more questions."

"Absolutely."

"Great, thanks! It may seem like an odd question, but during our conversation you mentioned that the day Jim passed, it was one of the best days of his life. Can you walk me through that?"

"Yes, believe it or not it was one of the best days of his life. Seriously, it was. We had coffee together that morning and visited for a bit. He got his teasing in and then he dropped me off and picked me up from work so we could have lunch together. Then he went fishing. You know how much Jim loved to fish. He caught five and brought them home, filleted them, and then planned on giving them away to one of our friends.

"For supper, I made him his favorite meal of hamburger soup and bannock. That night after supper, he came over and kissed me on the forehead for some reason. He rarely did that. He thanked me for making his favorite meal and then he retreated to the living room to bury his backside in his favorite recliner. I told him I was heading to church, so he said goodbye and then picked up his beloved Sudoku game and began playing. It was the best day of his life. He got to do everything he loved to do all in one day. I am so thankful for that."

What a reflection! What a perspective! I know it hasn't been easy for her, and I know there will be some additional days of struggle, but it was so nice to see that her thankfulness, combined with the fruits of her labor, helped her to find better days.

"It makes me happy knowing you're on the mend and that Jim had such an amazing last day," I said. "Throughout your life and your recent loss, how would you say being thankful has helped you, and what are you most thankful for?"

"Honestly, it has been a very difficult three years. His memories definitely carry me through the tougher days. Thank God for memories! Sometimes I feel like he is here, and that helps. I've also realized I am so much better if I'm caring for others. Volunteering and giving back definitely helps. Jim was like that. It's like I'm taking him along with me. He always gave to others. The gift of his hands, his time, and his humor. For that I am eternally grateful. When I used to get worked up, Jim would let me have my moments, but if it went on too long he would say, 'Enough.' Sternly. In other words, 'Be thankful. Things could be worse.' He was so right. Nothing is that important. I am thankful I was gifted forty-seven years. I miss my Jimmy, but those memories keep me going!"

Memories are a vital part of life and are an important part in being able to be thankful. Life isn't always fair, but like Dora has taught us, memories combined with a thankful heart can help us to move forward! Her story is such a great teaching on being thankful for life's moments with the ones we love.

Dora followed up with me several weeks after the interview to make sure I had what I needed and to reiterate that I was always welcome in her home. You can rest assured I will be taking her and Jim up on that offer.

On another note, Dora, I can't close off your story without saying thank you for being willing to share your healing process with others. Jim would be so proud of his much "older" wife.

Chapter Six
Who Dances Around

When I was a young boy, breakdancing happened to be the latest and greatest craze for the younger generation. It was so popular that it seemed you couldn't go to any mall or turn on any TV channel without seeing all types of people performing or practicing this new type of artistic expression. From spinning on their heads to sliding across the floor, people danced without fear. In those moments, it was as if nothing could touch them. Dancing set them free from whatever may have been going on in their world at the time.

Around the same time as I was reflecting on one of my favorite childhood memories, I received a message from my best friend's mother informing me that her daughter—a.k.a. Bird—had recently received disheartening medical news and that she may be a good person to talk to for my book.

That unexpected news really frustrated me! Why do the nicest and kindest people often seem to get the short end of the stick? I knew there was no good answer to my questions, so instead of chasing them I chose to begin the process of quieting my thoughts by looking for the good. Within minutes, my frustration began to subside and was replaced with my inner voice saying to me, *Call her. You need to call her.* So I listened to my gut, picked up the telephone, and called her.

"Derek, how the heck are you?" she said, answering the phone. "Mom said you may be calling. I'm so glad you called. I have so much to share with you. Tell me about what you're doing. It sounds awesome! I got to say, I have so much to be thankful for."

Here was a woman who had recently lost all her hair and was in the throes of radiation and chemotherapy treatment, yet she was saying she had so much to be thankful for. This was the opposite of what I had expected. The last time I checked, chemo and radiation weren't the happiest of experiences. I wondered if she was being fully transparent or if she really did feel that way.

"Sorry to hear you're going through such a hard time, Bird. Your positive response caught me off-guard. Do you really feel that way?"

"That's funny. My doctor asked me a similar question. I guess I'm too happy or something. Honestly, I am good. Really good! Not sure what my mom told you, but while I was in Manitoba this summer I discovered a tumor in my breast that began to grow very fast and was extremely painful. The doctors sent me for additional testing and it turned out to be a cancerous tumor. I've lived with this lump for well over twenty years with no previous concerns. I've had it checked out yearly with non-cancerous results every time—until this year. My test results also showed that the lymph nodes under my arm 'did not look good.' I just had a bilateral mastectomy and I'm a little tired, but other than that, I'm pretty good."

Holy shitake mushrooms with a side of toast! Who talks with such positivity and conviction when they've recently lost both of their breasts? Who says they're good when they are literally going through hell?

Bird, that's who! It didn't take me long to figure out that there was a life lesson embedded in all of this: being thankful is an intentional choice.

"From as far back as I can remember, you have always been a positive person," I said. "I'm not sure why I doubted you. I do believe you now! I know you're a tough cookie, Bird, but at first was it a little tough to hear the C-word?"

"I'm not going to lie. Yes, it was especially tough in the beginning. When my doctor informed me of the cancer diagnosis, I cried. I cried a lot, actually. My life had just turned upside-down, but I knew I had a choice in how I would respond. I stood up in my living room, cranked up the stereo really loud, and danced. I put the song on repeat and kept dancing with tear-filled eyes until my husband got up and danced with me. We cried together. Oh what a time we had! Sounds crazy, but that is what I did. It is a moment in my life I will never forget, but it's also a time I now cherish and am totally thankful for. I knew I had to release my negative emotions if I was going to move forward through this journey with strength and positivity. After that, I made up my mind to do what my dad has always taught me: I prayed. I stayed thankful for what God has done and would do in my life and told myself, 'There is no way I will let cancer defeat me! I will not die. I will live.'"

I love that she knows she's in a fight but refuses to let her circumstance control her. It's one thing to be able to train yourself to be positively focused but a whole other thing to believe it fully and know enough to actively be thankful and speak what you want into your life.

"You are an amazing human being, Bird. I love how you're staying true to who you are and your faith! It's inspiring. Were there any defining moments or turning points that helped you along the way?"

"Thanks. I appreciate that. You know, it all became real when I slowly started losing my hair. It was a tough pill to swallow. I've had long hair most of my life, but at some point while grieving I came to the conclusion that it could be worse. I could be six feet under. So I made a choice to shave it all off. Believe it or not, it was one of the happiest days of my journey because it helped me to start taking my thought life back."

What a revelation of truth. She may have had cancer, but she also knew it had no control over how she would choose to confront its attempts to steal her joy. It wasn't easy, but nothing worth fighting for ever is.

"Your attitude of gratitude towards what you're going through needs to be shared."

"Thanks. I'm actually putting some things together to share with others of what has helped me and what I have learned. It is a passion of mine for sure."

What an amazing woman! If you ask me, it's an incredible kindness to pull together information to help others while in the middle of radiation treatments.

"You never cease to amaze me with your willingness to help others. Warms my heart, Bird. Can we talk a bit more about some of your turning points? You said losing your hair was a big one for you. Was there anything else that reshaped your thinking?"

"Yes. There was another really big one for me. Probably the biggest, actually. I was at home waiting for a call from my doctor about my pathology test results and my phone rang, and I knew it was her—so I answered it. We had some small talk and then she began talking about my results. The pathology report had come back and the large breast lump was malignant, but there were no cancerous cells in the margin around the tumor. The other great news was that the lymph nodes removed during surgery had tested negative. Cancer had not spread to the lymph nodes. I was so happy. I had told her that my lymph nodes would come back negative. I'd believed and prayed for that. I was so thankful. I hung up the phone and decided that this called for another dance around my living room, thanking God for answering my prayer."

What a lesson on finding joy and strength where and whenever available. Yes, she had malignant tumors but she chose instead to focus on the good news of her lymph node tests coming back cancer-free.

Even more eye-opening was how she celebrated, with not one but two victory booty shakes while still in the middle of the battle for her life. Dumbfounded by her approach, I found my inner self asking questions like, *Who dances around after they've been told they have malignant tumors? Who celebrates in the middle of their big-C circumstance?*

The answer that came back loud and clear was this: someone who realizes that life is a gift! Whether it's a warm building with a soft sofa or a good old-fashioned booty shake, we all have so much to be thankful for.

"When you know God loves you and you're thankful for what you have in your life, you can deal with whatever experience you're going through. Something absolutely happened when I surrendered to that way of thinking. I felt totally empowered. I knew I would beat it and I've never looked back."

"I know now why your mom told me to call you," I said. "You truly represent what it means to be thankful in all things. I know you're still going through treatments, but I want you to know that I'm here for you if you need me. And I'll be praying for your full recovery as well."

"Thank you. I appreciate that. People need to know there is hope!"

"You got that right. I know we've talked for longer than I said this would take, but I'm so glad we did. I just have one last question I need to ask: when you think back on your situation and throughout your life, what are you most thankful for? And how has being thankful helped you get to where you are today?"

"When I look back over my life and my experience with cancer, the first thing that comes to my mind is how my faith and trust in God helped me through my difficult times. During chemo treatments, I remember just lying there with the energy totally sucked out of me. I couldn't stop coughing, which meant I didn't sleep. I felt like I'd been run over a few hundred times by the biggest truck out there. But in those rough moments, I also remember how I just kept thinking, *I'm so thankful I am alive.* When my mind and thoughts were under attack, my faith protected me from being defeated. Like I told my doctor, I don't know how a 'normal' cancer patient would respond, but I know I have much to be thankful for. There was no way I was going to let cancer take that from me. I can honestly say I am a very different person now, and in a good way. I'm definitely more thankful for each and every day. I know now more than ever that there is so much to be grateful for! Being thankful is a big part of who I am today."

Bird's thankful, dancing approach to the unfair cancer diagnosis she received helped her get through her darkest hours. It wasn't easy to do but, like she said, there is so much to be grateful for.

Chapter Seven
The Gift of Circumstance

I first met Gina several years ago when I was fortunate to travel with her to the launch of an innovative education partnership agreement between a First Nation and the provincial school system. It was late in the day and the event was a five-hour drive.

To complicate matters, Mr. Canadian Winter (CW) and his twin brats, Ms. Howling Wind and Mr. Blowing Snow, had hoped to discourage us from making the trip. However, this wasn't our first rodeo, so we blew off their fear tactics and headed out to face the storm.

Apparently our decision annoyed them. For the next two hours Mr. CW's children came at us harder than Donald Trump's idiotic tweets, but to no avail. The brats didn't understand there wasn't a snowball's chance in hell we would give in to their pressure so easily.

Mr. CW must have caught wind of the brats' unsuccessful attempts to disrupt our "never give up, never give in" attitude, because within an hour of reaching our destination the storm mysteriously vanished into thin air.

For those of you who are thinking I may be a few bricks short of a load, rest assured I'm fully aware that this is just an analogy. All joking aside, the drive turned out to be an accurate reflection of the trip.

"Hi Derek," Gina said. "Thanks for including me in this project. I will give you what I can. I hope it helps you to fulfill what you're doing. I really like the concept!"

"Thanks Gina, and thank you for accepting my invitation to do the interview by phone. I know you're super busy, so how about we dive right into this?

"Ask away."

"Thank you. Okay. How about we start with where you grew up?"

"I spent the better part of my childhood on the Kitigan-Zibi First Nation. My dad was in the military, and my mom stayed home to raise me and my brother. She was young and had me when she was just a teenager. We didn't have running water at times and money was scarce, but we always had the basic necessities. I just remember being happy."

In North America, material wealth and financial status are often portrayed by the media as indicators of people's personal happiness. However, it became clear to me that Gina hadn't enjoyed either of these things. Yet she remembered being happy.

I decided to ask what her determinates for "being happy" were.

"Well, some of my happiness came from those times I got to spend with my cousins hanging out at Cayer Lake, feeling connected to them, the land, and that area," she said. "With Dad away so much, I also got to spend a lot of quality time with my mom. She gave me so much attention, and that really made me happy. But probably my fondest memory is Mom reading to me every night. She rarely missed. I'm so thankful for that memory! It's definitely one that I hold on to."

Her response was such a great representation of the type of joy that can be experienced simply by choosing to be thankful. It also became abundantly clear to me that her ability to be happy had nothing to do with the superficial happiness indicators that lead us to believe we require things in order to be joyful. Her happiness was attached to people and moments rather than things. What a simple yet profound revelation of truth.

It hadn't occurred to me that choosing to be thankful could bring someone so much happiness. Completely absorbed by her way of thinking, I pressed on, hoping to discover a few more of her hidden teachings.

"Funny how memories work," I said. "I could actually feel your gratitude for those moments through the telephone. Especially when you shared about your mom reading to you. It sounds to me like your time with your cousins, your mom, and your earliest years are some of your most cherished moments. How about your teenage years? What were they like?"

"Those early years were pretty great, but in my teenage years my family life began to take a negative turn and I started to encounter some things that caused me to struggle. My parents' marriage ended and then Mom started drinking. At first it was occasionally, but it wasn't long before it began to own her. She was partying regularly and there were always people at our house. It wasn't healthy and I began to hate the environment I was in. I loved my community. I loved my mom. But she was at a point where it seemed that the only thing she was interested in was partying. I remember just wanting to graduate and get the hell out of there. Not off my reserve, but away from the environment of my home at the time."

So when the opportunity presented itself, Gina made the heart-breaking decision to leave her family so she could focus on completing her high school and postsecondary education.

"That must have been quite difficult for you," I said.

"It was, but at the time it was what I needed to do. I swore back then that I would never move back into that environment. It wasn't until several years later, when I was offered a job back in my First Nation, that I considered returning."

"Was it the Cayer Lake side of you that solidified your decision to return home?'

"For sure. All I know is that returning home was one of the best things I did. It allowed me to reconcile with myself. I was also given the opportunity by leadership to work in partnership with my community on some important initiatives they wanted to move forward on. That experience really taught me about people and life. It was during those years that I truly learned about being inclusive and making sure to consult thoroughly with people before making big decisions. The time I spent there definitely helped support me in becoming the leader I am today! I am truly thankful I returned home because it was one of those life experiences that has taught me so much."

Sometimes our best learning comes from facing the challenges that caused us uninvited pain. Listening to Gina share her story allowed me to better understand that successes in life not only come from God-given abilities but from the value you assign to those experiences. Fascinated again by her approach, I decided it was time to move my questions towards learning more about the lessons she'd learned from her senior leadership positions.

"So after working for your community, you ended up working for the Assembly of First Nations (AFN) National Chief. How did that happen?"

"Actually, I just applied. I went for it. I started as a policy analyst and over time I was able to work my way through the ranks. The AFN is such a dynamic organization. I really earned my political and strategic stripes there. Working in both my community and the AFN were very valuable lessons, for sure. They made me focus on the bigger picture and the impacts of my decisions!"

"Who would you say is or was your biggest leadership influencer?

"Definitely National Chief Ovide Mercredi. He taught me so much about leadership and strategy. I truly admire him for those lessons. I still admire him. He is partly who I model my leadership style after today."

As Gina continued telling me about her experiences with the AFN and the multitude of other leadership opportunities that helped raise her to one of the highest ranking federal offices in Canada, I couldn't help but notice a pattern in all her successes. No matter which experience or who we talked about, she always expressed her appreciation for the teachings she received. It was nice to see a leader of her stature show such a genuine spirit of thankfulness, especially because I also knew she had experienced more than her fair share of personal loss along the way.

"Gina, you shared earlier that your father and mother both passed away while you were only in your twenties, that your daughter was diagnosed with the same type of cancer Terry Fox had, and that you unexpectedly lost your husband to suicide due to his residential school experiences. You've had a lot of private heartbreak to deal with, yet you continue to thrive and find your way through it all. Most people would have given up or given in already. How did you do it? How do you remain so thankful? Seriously, how did you become a federal deputy minister after all that?"

"Tough, but good questions," she said. "Well, I definitely got through it in many different ways. Support from family, friends, and my beliefs definitely helped. It is important to recognize that circumstances have their gifts. Cancer taught me to not sweat the small stuff. I have my daughter, and thankfully she recovered. That was the worst year of my life. All I could think about was her. It's so hard when your child is in so much pain, and I knew I couldn't take it away. But you know, it also taught me a few other things. Death made me realize that I needed to be thankful for each and every moment I have on this earth, with the people I love, and to make sure I am more present with my loved ones. I definitely could have chosen to be bitter, but how would that have helped me or anybody else? There truly is so much to be thankful for.

"As for how did I become a deputy minister, I think anyone who rises in their career owes much to their upbringing and their life experiences, good or bad. Many of my colleagues had very positive childhood experiences—and easier lives than mine, I would think. Certainly not all, but many. For those who have had it more tough, I believe the challenges create accelerated learning opportunities. It is often said that as talented people develop in their careers, they need to get out of their comfort zone. I would say that I have encountered many points in life of discomfort to say the least."

Wow! What a perspective! What an absolutely amazing woman. They often say that when you're in the presence of greatness, you will know it. Not because someone tells you how good they are but because the gift of their character inspires you to do better and be better for others. I can say without hesitation that Gina is definitely a person of greatness to me.

"Thank you for agreeing to speak with me and for sharing some of your story for the project. It is such a great teaching that I believe many will benefit from. Before I let you go, can I ask you one last question?"

"Absolutely. I'm an open book. What would you like to know?"

"What are you most thankful for, and how has thankfulness played a role in your life?"

"I know I have experienced a lot of tough things, but I am thankful I can use those things to my advantage. They definitely have made me resilient. I'm thankful for each moment I have here with the ones I love. My grandmas! They were extremely strong role models. They loved you no matter what and showed it. I often think of them and am very thankful for those teachings. My grandmothers both had a hand in my discipline and didn't hold back on criticizing a wrongdoing. At the same time, they were both very affectionate and I felt loved and safe when I slept at their homes and would cuddle with them as I fell asleep. Their values shaped me with their sharp honesty and their loving kindness. I am thankful that my experiences in life have allowed me to help others. It's important to remember that you may experience suffering, but you also can find joy. It really is about being thankful for what we've been given."

As I hung up the telephone, I quickly recognized that besides the fact that Gina is an amazing leader, she is an even more amazing human being. Her story is such a great example of how a person can disallow the bite or wound of a snake (a person, event, or circumstance) from taking them out. Instead, use the gifts of those circumstances to help you create the way towards hope, healing, and your breakthrough.

Chapter Eight
One Day at a Time

Late one night, I received an email from a friend inviting me to attend a fundraising gala for an organization called Live Different, at the Canadian Museum for Human Rights in Winnipeg. Live Different is a charity that helps young people embrace a more caring lifestyle.

Grateful for the opportunity, I decided to arrive a bit early so I could take in the entire gala experience. Upon arrival, I began to walk around the venue to view the multitude of items that were up for auction. Immediately I was drawn to the photography section and the artistry that was on display. That was the first time I was introduced to Tracy.

"Isn't that photo amazing?" she said with the world's biggest smile. "I love it."

"Yes, the one with the child smiling is pretty cool."

"I agree. It is absolutely beautiful. It was taken by Cole Brown, the guy we are honoring tonight. I put in a bid for it—and if I win, you see that volunteer standing over there? I'm going to give it to him as a surprise. He really wants it."

Intrigued by her generosity, I continued to engage in our conversation.

"I see you have your WestJet outfit on, and I know they provide corporate sponsorship," I said. "Is that why you're here?"

"Well, kind of. They're my employer, but I would do it even if they weren't. I find volunteering to be so rewarding. It's something I have come to truly love doing. It probably helps me just as much as it helps others."

Her comment really grabbed hold of me. The longer we chatted, the more I became convinced that she probably had a story to tell.

"How often do you volunteer?" I asked. "Do you do the mission trips with Live Different?"

"As often as I can. I just came back from a mission trip. It was wonderful. I find it rejuvenates me and makes me so thankful for what I have. Especially since October 1."

What did she mean by that? Why was that date so important to her? My Spidey senses were tingling, but I knew this gala wasn't the time or place to dive into what appeared to be a deeply personal experience. Instead I decided to tell her about my book project and invite her to meet me at a later date to be part of it.

"Tracy, I know we just met, and this may sound odd—but I'm currently writing a book and my goal is to interview as many women as possible to see how being thankful has played a role in their lives. Based on our brief conversation, I think you may be a great candidate for what I'm doing. I can send you the outline and if you decide you are interested, we could arrange to meet. Thoughts?"

"You know what, that is very thought-provoking. I'm actually on a journey of healing myself. So yes, it may be something I would consider, but I would need a little more information and some time to think about it. Could I get back to you next week?"

"Absolutely. Either way, it was nice to talk with you. Enjoy the evening."

True to her word, the following week I received a message saying she would love to participate. Happy that my gut feeling had once again come through, I proposed a time and place and the rest is history!

"Thanks again for agreeing to meet with me," I said. "I definitely didn't think that by attending the gala I would end up meeting someone for my book. Life definitely works in mysterious ways."

"It sure does. Hope what I share is what you're looking for. How would you like to proceed?"

"It's just a conversation really. I take notes while we're talking, so don't mind me. I'll send back to you whatever I come up with—and if you like it, I'll add it to the others to use in a book someday. Sound good?"

"Sounds wonderful. I'm ready whenever you are."

"Perfect. I would like to explore something you said to me back at the gala. You said that volunteering has helped you, especially since October 1. What did you mean by that?"

With tears rolling down her cheeks, she began to tense up a bit. No words came out, but I could tell she was desperately trying to speak. A small panic entered my thoughts, as I hadn't expected this reaction. Nor did I know what to say. My "maleness" wanted to fix the situation, but my heart was telling me to shut up, wait, and listen.

"Sorry, it's still just a bit hard sometimes," she said. "I was… I was in Vegas during the Harvest Music Festival shootings. I was at that concert!"

I couldn't believe my ears. The Las Vegas concert shootings injured more than eight hundred people, and fifty-eight people lost their lives that day, not to mention the trauma others continue to experience as a result of the attack.

"I couldn't even imagine," I said. "Are you sure you want to do this?"

"Yes, I want to. I need to, actually! This is therapeutic for me. I'm slowly taking my life back and this seems like a good way to help me to do that!"

"Thank you for being so brave. If at any time you change your mind, let me know. Start wherever you want and go wherever your thoughts and heart take you."

"Where to start? Well, the belt buckle I was wearing that day said 'Wild Heart, Gypsy Soul.' I love it because it also doubles as a wallet and lets you be hands-free. Perfect for a venue like that. I work for WestJet, as you know, so the flights were really cheap and so was my room. It was supposed to be super nice out. What could go wrong, right? I was so excited for it, but as it turned out it was one of the worst days of my life."

Once again she began welling up, but this time it didn't seem to have the same power to stop her from saying what she needed to say. In a way, it was inspiring because I felt like she was having a small breakthrough simply by talking to me.

"Sorry for the tears," she said. "I'm still a work in progress. As I reflected on whether or not to participate in this project, I decided that if it can help someone else heal or have a breakthrough, then I'm in. I need to do this. Not just for me, but for others."

What a selfless act to be willing to share her traumatic life experience in hopes that it could help others. Her story was one I had never anticipated, but I'm so thankful she trusted me to record it.

"Can you walk me through that day?"

"It was such a gorgeous day! We took in the sights in the morning, and then later on in the day we decided to head to the Las Vegas Village where the concert was happening. The smell of barbeque from all the venues had filled the air. It smelled so amazing. We grabbed some food, a few drinks, and then sat on the bleachers to take it all in. It was so cool."

"Who was playing at the main stage at the time when the craziness happened? Do you remember that?"

"Yes, Jason Aldean! I remember thinking to myself that he sounded way better than I thought he would. I took out my phone and took a few pictures. That's the last thing I can remember doing before the shooting began. People were screaming and running everywhere. It was a scary scene." Pausing to take a deep breath, she smiled at me and took a sip of her coffee. "My eyes were closed and I was lying facedown on the ground. I was terrified by all the screams I was hearing. I froze. I could hear the bullets ricocheting all around me but I couldn't move. I just froze. I had never experienced that before, nor do I ever want to again."

Truth be told, I couldn't believe what I was hearing. In fact, I felt so guilty about her having to relive those traumatic moments that I wanted to stop the interview. However, because she had reassured me that our discussion was cathartic, and because she'd stated multiple times that she was no longer prepared to let that circumstance control her, I decided to continue on.

"Were you hurt?" I asked. "How did you find the strength to get off the ground and run to safety?"

"No, I wasn't hurt, but I was terrified. I could see that others around me had been injured. I just laid there, because I still couldn't find the courage to get up and run. I was so scared! The bullets were flying everywhere—and then it went quiet for a moment. He must have been reloading. I could hear the guy behind me yelling at his wife or girlfriend, 'Get up. We got to get the hell out of here.' So I joined them. It was hard, but I somehow forced myself to get up and run. I didn't get very far before the bullets were bouncing all around me again. The next thing I knew, I was back on my face, panicking because bullets were flying all over the place and coming in our direction again."

Silence was trying to force its way back into our conversation, but she was having no part of it. With the strength of a warrior, she shook off whatever fears were pushing against her and spoke with confidence.

"I told myself, if I'm going to die, I'm going to die trying. I knew I could do it, I just needed a little extra help. So I prayed and asked God to give me the strength and protection I needed to get to safety. Immediately after I did it, a strange sense of calmness came over me. I wasn't scared anymore. All I know is that it gave me the courage to run. I just remember running and running and running until I got to a fence. A guy helped me get over it. I continued to run into one of the casinos. It was at that point I finally felt that I was safe."

Thankfully, she was able to find the inner strength to get up and run. Thankfully, she decided that one way or another she would overcome her circumstance. Thankfully, she decided that she would rather die trying than let what was happening take her out.

Does she have a moment once in a while? Absolutely! Does that day still bother her from time to time? You bet! But the more important question is this: does that moment in her life own her anymore? No way!

"You are truly an amazing woman," I said. "I'm amazed at what you went through and at how you are rebuilding you again."

"Thank you. *One day at a time* is my motto. I still struggle a bit, but I am definitely better."

"How do you know?"

"I know because I was able to go back to Las Vegas for the one-year anniversary. I decided I needed to face it head-on. I also knew I needed to be with others who had experienced what I did. I went back because I'm not going to let fear *control me*. That was an important step towards my healing."

As I sat in absolute awe, I was both amazed and saddened by what had been brought into her life. I was also inspired by how resourceful and determined she was to regain what had been stolen from her. Survival was not the only option. She deserved way more than that, and from what I could tell her efforts were slowly but surely paying off.

"Thank you for sharing your story with me and the world. I didn't expect it, but man is there a world of healing, hope, and breakthrough buried in there."

"Thank you for asking. This has been quite therapeutic for me. Talking is good!"

"My pleasure. I know we both need to get going, but I'd like to ask one last question to close off the interview. Throughout your life, how has thankfulness helped you and what are you most thankful for?"

"I am so thankful I went back to Las Vegas to be with other survivors. One of the best parts of me returning there was when I visited the healing garden. That experience was something else! I met a parent there who had lost her son. She spoke with me and during our conversation she said to me that I am here for a reason, a purpose, and that I was meant to stay here on earth. That really made me think. It's one of the things that continues to help me to move forward. It helped me to start to look and believe in the greater good again. I got to take back a part of me that was lost for a while. It has allowed me to see what I do have in my life. I'm so thankful for that.

"My husband was and is my rock through all this. I'm so thankful for him! I didn't think there was a man on earth like him until this happened to me. I'm also very thankful for my pets. They have helped me walk again. I'm thankful for my country. The customs guy hugged me when I got home and welcomed me back to Canada. It woke me up. Changed my perspective. Made me realize there are good people out there. Life is so worth living! It opened me up to the fact that I do matter and that I need to make sure I take better care of myself! I'm grateful for my grandchildren and the opportunity to be a part of their lives. I'm thankful that this may help other people. This may have shaken me in lots of ways, but I have truly become more thankful."

Her story is such a courageous example of not allowing a tragic circumstance or experience to stop you from living your life. Granted, it has taken Tracy time and effort to work through the trauma from that terrible day, but her one-day-at-a-time approach is helping her get to better days.

Chapter Nine
The Treasure in Memories

Years ago, I provided a chapter from my book, *Don't Blame the Children* (unpublished at the time) to Professor Karen Rempel to read and give me her thoughts. With tears in her eyes, she looked at me and said, "I absolutely love it. Let me know when you get it published. I would like a copy." Her confidence in my writing gave me the boost I needed to keep pressing on with it.

So needless to say, when I created my shortlist of people to ask to participate in this project, her name was at the top of my list.

"Are you ready for this?" Karen asked, staring at me as if I had no idea what I was getting into.

"I'm actually looking forward to it," I replied. "Thank you for accepting."

"I see you're not recording me, so slow me down if you can't keep up with your notes. I get carried away. I tend to do that." She chuckled.

"I'll keep that in mind. What was it like growing up? Mountaintops? Valleys?"

"Well, to put it nicely, it was mostly valleys. When I was nine years old, I became the mother to my brothers. Dad was busy drinking all the time. My earliest memories of my father are not hugs or fun family gatherings. You know what it was? It was him stumbling around our home… drunk. He was never much of a father. Nice enough guy, but not a father. He drank every day from the time I could recall."

"That must have been hard. What about your mom?

"Mom was a beautiful woman. She had a model/movie star appearance. Because of that, I'm sure many assumed she had it all together, but internally she was completely unhappy with her life. She rarely engaged in any family functions and was stone-faced most of the time. She wasn't able to express her feelings in any meaningful way. It incapacitated her to he point that I don't remember a time when she was emotionally available to us."

I'd had no idea the first part of our conversation would reveal Karen had grown up truly parentless. She'd obviously made some sort of peace with her past and I wanted to know how she had done it.

"You were a child yourself. I couldn't imagine having to deal with all that," I said. "It sounds like life was far from easy or fair for you in your early life. How did you get through those undeserving times? What helped you to find your way?"

"All I knew was that someone needed to step up and look after the family, so I did everything and anything that was needed to make sure we were taken care of. It was just that simple. I also tended to find people and things that brought me hope and held onto them. You know, I remember a family moving in across the street from us. They were such a nice family. I became really close friends with their daughter Annie and they helped me realize that family could be different. I spent a lot of time around them and I'm grateful for that."

"Have you ever seen the family or Annie since then? It would be kind of cool for you to share with them what you know now."

"I haven't, but you're right. It would be nice to at least acknowledge the importance of their family in my life. Who knows? One day maybe! You know, besides them, the biggest influence in my life wasn't a person but a place. It started with my grandma's farm… "

I waited for her to finish, but she had looked away and trailed off into a reflective pause.

"I'd love to tell you about how the farm influenced my life," she continued after a while. "As I look back, it wasn't the farm in particular but the rolling hills and prairie landscape. Even though I grew up in the city, we lived very close to where there was still native prairie grasslands. As I learned more about my grandmother and great-grandmother, I came to believe that I may have gotten my love of the prairies from them—and perhaps also my tenacity. For example, my great-grandmother had lots of trials and tribulations. She actually immigrated from Russia to the U.S. with her husband, but after they arrived her husband passed away unexpectedly. Somehow she ended up in Canada and established a homestead on the prairies in a time when women still didn't have the right to vote. She also raised five children on her own. She had such a perseverance. She was a bit of a firecracker and a pioneer, I would say."

"Sounds like a pretty incredible woman! Do you think she helped you get to where you are today?"

"Without a doubt. I love to think about her and my grandmother as resilient women. Thinking about the things they went through has helped me get to where I am today."

Pausing once again, she took a long sip of her drink. As I waited for her to continue, I reflected on how impressed I was with her outlook on life. Most would have complained about that type of upbringing, but she was a silver-lining thinker.

Intrigued by her perspective, I decided to probe a bit into her trials. "You're such a positive person, but I'm guessing you had to work through a few things. Is that correct?"

"Yes, but I know that where there is a will, there is a way. Yes, I've had some challenges—a dysfunctional childhood, a failed marriage, near bankruptcy, health issues, family crises—but I've been able to put one foot ahead of the other and keep going."

"Wow, Karen, you've been to hell and back, so to speak. I never would have guessed. I'm captivated by your unrelenting determination and resilience. With all that adversity, how were you able to get to where you are today?"

"Good question! Getting my education. I've always loved to learn, and I knew that pursuing it would help me get out of the dysfunction I was in. It was a no-brainer, really. I just needed to find a way to achieve my goal. Also, I'm a bit of a risktaker. So I simply enrolled and went back to school, taking summer classes, night classes, and selling cattle on the side to make ends meet. I guess I just did it. I found a way to make it happen!"

Instead of focusing on her circumstance, she had consciously made the choice to employ her grandma's tenacity. Not once during our conversation did she say it was easy, but she did say it was worth it.

"Thank you for sharing your story with me today," I said. "You are a true inspiration and a role model."

"Thank you, that's very kind."

"I would like to ask you one final question, Karen. When you look back, how would you say thankfulness has played a role in your life? And what are you most thankful for?"

"Well, I don't think you or anyone can survive without being thankful. Every time you meet a challenge, you can say it's really sh#!ty, or you can say the cup is still half full! It's always half full in my mind. Nothing is insurmountable unless you allow it to be. I am truly thankful that I can see the world that way."

It's in the intentional, habitual looking for things to be thankful for that we are able to form a more positive outlook in any situation. Granted, it may not be easy at the start to do, but it's definitely worth the effort.

Chapter Ten
A Beautiful Exchange

For quite some time, I had been teasing my friend Nonie about allowing me to interview her for the Thankfulness Project. For weeks she would say, "I don't really have much of a story, but let me think about it. Ask me next week." Normally, I would have given up, but in this case something was telling me she did have a story, so I continued asking, hoping she would change her mind.

Eventually that day did come, but not before she made sure to say to me loudly, "Okay, see you Saturday… but like I said before, and I'm just warning you, you're probably going to leave disappointed."

It would be a lie to say Nonie's reluctance didn't make me question my inclination to interview her. However, my gut told me I needed to follow through, so I parked my doubts and attended our scheduled meeting.

As it turned out, the story she shared was one of the most perspective-shifting, forgiving thankfulness stories I've had the pleasure of hearing.

"Thanks for agreeing to help me with this, Nonie. And thanks for supper. It was great! Are you ready to do this?"

"You're welcome. I'm ready whenever you are. I see you've been busy. Your journal looks like it's just about full. Remember, though, I'm not sure I have much of a story to share."

Again, she put that caveat out there. I didn't want to pry, but she wouldn't have agreed to talk with me if she hadn't wanted to. So I decided to go back in time with her and see how she had become the successful woman she was.

"Let's just chat for a bit and see where we end up. If there is no story, then at least we had a good conversation. How about starting with your childhood? What was it like? Where did you go to school?"

The response I received back wasn't what I expected.

"Well, you know I spent time in the foster care system, right?"

As soon as she said it, I understood exactly why she was so reserved about putting her story in written form for all the world to see. A little taken aback, I offered to take our conversation in a different direction.

"No," she immediately said. "It needs to be talked about. I'm ready. It's time!"

"How long where you in care? How old where you?"

Tears began to roll down her cheeks. "As a little girl, my mother and father weren't fully involved in my life. I spent my early childhood in and out of foster homes up until I was eight years old. Some were good, others not so much. There are good people in that field, too. My longest placement in care was pretty good. That foster mother cared about me and I felt that. The affection was there, but it's just not the same as a mom and dad's love."

As soon as she finished, silence filled the room. I could see how those experiences had impacted her. She wanted to speak, but in that moment no words would come out.

"Nonie, I'm sorry. We don't need to talk about that part of your life. Let's move on."

"No, I'm fine. I just haven't talked about this in forever. Honestly, I'm okay. It obviously needs to happen. I know I said I don't have a story, but I do. Being in care was really hard—not because of the families I was placed with, but because both my mom and dad were alive. Because of their circumstances, they were unable to care for me. They had things they needed to work through. As a little girl, I understood that as best I could, but at times I also felt unwanted."

How heartbreaking. To say her circumstance had been unfair would be an understatement. I couldn't imagine the emotional struggles she had endured throughout those years. It would be distressing enough not having parents, but to know they were out there and unable to care for you? I was glad she was allowing me to write her story, but also saddened by it.

"Sorry, Nonie, that must have been really hard on you. I would have never known or guessed. I honestly had no idea. You are always so positive and happy. Would you say that's because you've been able to grieve that part of your life?"

"Yes. I'm in a good place today. Just thinking back on those things can be hard, I guess. I have definitely moved forward and I'm thankful I was able to come to terms with it. Now that I'm an adult, I get why my dad wasn't able to care for me back then."

"Did your dad or mom ever get to a spot where they could take care of you?"

"Yes, my dad did," she said. "I remember the day he came to get me for good. I was so happy. Even when he promised me I would never go back into care, I couldn't shake the fearful feeling inside me that I could end up back in care, so I did whatever I was told. I always knew he loved me and did experience his love every day after I left foster care. He honestly was a great dad, but the go-back-into-care feelings stayed with me until I became an adult."

I sat there thinking about how small any of my own circumstances were compared to what she had experienced. Her resilience and ability to accept these unfair situations was truly remarkable. I needed to know what had helped her to overcome that time in her life.

"Nonie, your experiences as a little girl were challenging in so many ways. How did you find the strength to reconcile your past?"

"If I'm being honest, I would say my dad's daily showing of love was important. It definitely helped to shape me into who I am today." She smiled. "But it's the gift my biological mom gave me that is the real story helping me to move on."

Up until this point in our conversation, we had done a fair amount of talking about her father, but almost nothing about her mom. I was happy I would finally learn more about her and about the important contribution she had made to Nonie's life.

"Tell me about her," I said. "What was she like? Did you have a relationship with her after you came out of care?"

"My biological mom lived a hard life because of her experience in residential school, and she had recovered from drug and alcohol abuse. I never really got to know her until a few months before she passed away from cancer. We cried and shared stories. I forgave her, and after that we really connected like a mother and daughter. She told me that her demons had gotten the best of her and that she hadn't been able to care for me. There was no way she was going to let me experience her hell. So she allowed me to be in care. I'm so amazed that she loved me so much that she was willing to give me up. If she hadn't, my life definitely would have been different. I am very thankful for her decision and the time I got to spend with her."

Again I was caught off-guard by her response. Nonie definitely had walked a rougher road than I had, but she was one of the kindest, most caring and giving women I'd ever met. It was so impressive to see how she had chosen to find the good in her circumstance and become better instead of bitter. What a great example of forgiveness! What an amazing example of unconditional love! What a beautiful exchange of love between a mother and daughter!

"Thank you for sharing this with me and allowing me to write about it," I said.

"I guess it was ready to come out. Been a long time! I'm glad you asked and I hope it helps whoever needs to hear it. As you know, there are definitely a lot of children in a worse situation than I was!"

"Yes, I hear you. Thanks again for supper and for doing this. Before I get going, I have one final questions for you. What are you most thankful for and how has being thankful helped you in your life?"

"I'm most thankful for my family—my dad, my mom, and of course my son—but I can honestly say that my biological mom's decision has made me into the mother and woman I am today. I am most thankful for her decision and her love. As for how being thankful has helped me throughout my life, it's helped me to experience great loss and great joy with an openness to learning from both of those types of moments. I'm still learning that it's normal to rely on other people in my life, and that it's okay to expect to be able to rely on others but at the same time remain thankful for the blessings I've already been given. It has enabled me to be a good friend and be a good person to those who need a good person in their life."

Often people have a hard time accepting, reciprocating, or receiving unconditional love. However, like Nonie and her mother, when we do, it becomes such a beautiful exchange!

Chapter Eleven
Fear Not

I first met Stephanie in the early nineties when she was travelling with her family for their music ministry. She was passionate about singing, and it would be an understatement to say she was talented. Unfortunately, we lost touch for a while. But through the sometimes-gift of social media, I was able to reconnect with this small-town girl from New Brunswick who'd enjoyed some success in the Christian music industry.

"Hey Steph, I'm so happy we're finally able to do this! Thanks for making the time. I know that with your five children, helping pastor a church, and your music ministry, you are one busy woman."

"It's my pleasure," she said. "I'll give you anything I can."

"Feel free to share as little or as much as you feel comfortable with. I was hoping to start with your musical journey. How old were you when you first discovered you could sing?"

"I was pretty young. I loved to sing at home. We sang in our living room a lot as a family and we began to tour across Canada and the U.S. when I turned eleven. As I got older, Dad and Mom transitioned me into the lead vocalist for our family group."

"They obviously knew what the rest of us now know: you have a vocal gift."

"Thank you. I knew I could sing, but transitioning to lead vocalist scared me. I found it really hard. For some reason it made me tense. It made me scared to go on stage in public. My stage fright was so bad that it would stop me from reaching the vocal notes I wanted and needed."

"Do you remember how you overcame that obstacle, or did it just go away?"

"It didn't go away on its own. I struggled for quite a bit with it, especially as a child and in my early teen years. Then, at a concert, my dad preached a perfectly timed message on choosing faith over fear. I had heard him talk about faith before, but this time it really hit home with me, and in my heart I responded to the call to live in faith instead of fear. After that, whenever I got tense, I would think about what he said. Since that sermon, I have never looked back."

We went on to talk about the power of words, about how we often miss that our beliefs about them often play a part in determining our emotional experiences. Steph was wise enough to choose to believe and put into action the words her dad spoke about faith—thankfully, otherwise we wouldn't be blessed with listening to her six top-ten hits on Christian radio.

"Well, I would say you have done remarkably well with beating the fear of being on stage. Remember when we randomly ran into one of the producers for the Newsboys at a music festival and you lost it?"

She laughed. "I do! Good memory. That was a total answer to prayer. Yes, God has been good to me!"

"I also remember you saying that one day you dreamed you'd be on stage like the artists at that music festival. To me, that's another great example of you choosing to have faith and believing you would one day achieve it. It probably didn't happen the way you envisioned, but that doesn't matter. What matters is that it did come to pass. Can we talk a little bit about how it all came together for you?"

"Absolutely, and I agree that faith and believing did play a major role in me achieving my goals. As funny as this may sound, one of my breaks came when I entered a singing contest in Barrie, Ontario called

Karaoke Superstar. I won it and it helped me land my first single, 'Lead Me There,' which did fairly well in Canada. After that, things really started to take off. I toured with World Vision and opened for numerous larger acts. I visited Nashville and met so many talented folks. Later I found myself writing new music and working in the studio on my own album!"

Her music began reaching people as her career flourished, with the amazing support of her family through it all. Even though she had those successes, though, she shared that on occasion she found herself feeling unhappy. Fear had held her back in her young life, and I wondered if that was the case again.

"I felt like that off and on when I was growing up. It wasn't all the time, but it was there. In my late twenties and early thirties, those unhappy feelings came into my life a bit more frequently. I had so many things going on. I had experienced a very personal loss, my husband and I had three rambunctious boys, and my musical ministry was keeping me busy. It was a stressful time in my life. I did eventually get through it."

I wanted to pursue these experiences when she felt unhappy, but instead decided to move on. I knew that if it was something that needed to be written into her story, she would let me know.

"Wow, that's a lot for anyone to handle," I said. "You were one busy mom."

"It was. And yes, I was. Thankfully, my family is amazingly supportive and I had my faith during those times."

"How did you end up back in New Brunswick? It's not exactly a musical hotbed," I said jokingly.

"I know, right? In the business of it all, I started to feel like it was time to make a change. Both my husband and I were feeling a draw to move back to New Brunswick, but my thoughts were holding me back. I guess I kind of feared I would have to give up my music career. I knew the opportunities I was getting didn't come around every day, but I also knew the feeling I had to make a change in my spirit was too strong to ignore."

"So what did you do?"

"I shared what I was feeling with my husband, and he was very supportive. He is such a blessing and an amazing man. We prayed about it and we decided it was time to move on to the next season in our lives. We moved to New Brunswick and began to work in church ministry."

"Good for you for not giving into fear," I said. "Not a lot of people would have done that. Did you ever ask yourself, 'Why am I moving back to New Brunswick where record labels aren't exactly on every street corner?'"

"In the beginning, I questioned the move, but my heart continued to confirm for me that it had been the right decision. Ironically, it wasn't long after we arrived in New Brunswick that an opportunity came up for me to record another album. I actually won my second GMA award, Female Vocalist of the Year, that year. And I opened for Mercy Me!"

By not seeing fear as a permanent part of her mindset, but rather as an obstacle in her way of thinking, she had been able to manage her thought life more effectively. This gave her the courage to act on what she felt she needed to do.

The results speak for themselves. Fear had lost its grip and faith won her another victory.

"This has been such a good teaching on confronting your fears," I said.

"Before we wrap things up, though, there's something I've been wanting to say," she said. "Because of our discussion, I'm realizing that I've been letting fear hold me back in another way. I have experienced a slight depression. I know that I've been so blessed along the way, and I'm truly thankful for those moments, but if I'm being completely honest, I have also struggled at times."

"Are you sure you want me to write this into your story, Steph?"

"Yes, please go ahead and use it. If it helps someone, then I'm happy. I feel like someone needs to hear that part of my life. We all go through things and I am no different."

"Thank you for being willing to be so vulnerable," I said. "Earlier in our conversation, you told me how your dad preached a sermon that helped you overcome your stage fright. Did he speak a word into your life again? Or was there anyone else or any other experience that helped you through those times of struggle?"

"The love and support I received from my dad and family played a big part in confronting the sadness I felt. There was also a singer in Nashville who brought me a lot of inspiration and strength. But it's important to me for people to know that without my faith, praise and worship, and my trust in Jesus Christ, I never would have gotten through any of it."

People are often hesitant to share what they believe has helped them because of the fear of what people may say or think. I'm so glad Steph gave the response she did. Hope, healing, and breakthroughs can come in many ways and faith is certainly one of them!

"I appreciate your honesty, Steph. Can you tell me a little more about how the singer in Nashville brought you inspiration?"

"Absolutely. She was a well-known woman in music ministry and I had always looked up to her as a child. One day, I learned she'd had a few bouts of depression. I felt I could relate to her story as a ministry person and as someone growing up in a travelling musical family. She shared that at the pinnacle of her depression she had been invited by a caring friend to help out in the inner city. When she got there, she discovered that she would be serving soup to less fortunate people. It had been a real eye-opener for her, helping her to refocus and remember that she had so much in her life to be thankful for. Hearing her story did the same for me."

We often get caught up in what we're missing instead of being thankful for what we do have in our lives. Love, friendship, a roof over our heads can easily be overlooked, but the truth is that the more you choose to appreciate, the more life will give you things to appreciate.

"Steph, before I let you go, I have one final question for you. What would you say you are most thankful for, and how has it helped you throughout your life?"

"I'm so thankful for people who help others or help in general. You can help by something you say or do, and you can be a light in those dark places. People and relationships are so important. Being thankful has helped me to recognize that. I'm completely thankful for my family. They keep me grounded. I am thankful for the blessing of all my friends and family along the way. Being thankful in all things has truly helped me in all that I do in my life."

After our conversation, I received an email in which Steph confided to me that there was a little more to her struggle, and she wanted to confront it head-on:

> I just want to thank you for last night and your heart and love for people. You made the interview easy. I really appreciate you. I also just want to add something to our conversation. Here is what I guess I really didn't touch fully on last night—the whole depression thing. I know so many people deal with it, so if this can help, I want to say it.
>
> I feel as though I've dealt with it my whole life. Actually, it's been just over a year that I've finally felt completely free! My doctor never diagnosed me as clinically depressed, but I know if I had opened up to her she would have helped me with medication. But for me, I know it was all in my perspective of the experiences of life. As a child, people saw the glory of ministry and traveling, which for me was amazing and I wouldn't change any of it, but the struggle was all too real at the same time, including financial struggle and disappointments.
>
> It's so easy for people to live from a place of disappointments. We can gauge our entire view of life from that place, instead of from the place of thankfulness. The true tragedy of walking through disappointments is that some people never leave that place. They stay there and bitterness can set in and the beauty of life and love can just dissipate and be gone.
>
> I would encourage those who deal with the type of depression that's not necessarily chemical but experiential to make the decision to walk away from the disappointments and look to life, love, and a thankful heart. Yes, they can be free! I've experienced it and I love the feeling of freedom and focusing on others and loving them.
>
> This past year, God has taught me so much about love. He is love. When we speak the name of God, you could just speak the word love because that's who and what He is. I love how He loves me and how He loves others through me!

Love you, brother, I will be praying for you and your project. I pray this book helps to set so many people free.

I have come to learn that as humans, we all struggle things that are big and small. So why would Steph be any different? The truth is that unhealthy fear comes in so many forms. I'm not talking about the type that enters your spirit when someone points a gun at you. I'm talking about unhealthy, thought-produced, wrongly defined fears.

For some, it is believing that they are not good enough. For others, it can be as small as worrying about making a mistake.

Unhealthy fears can be defeated by its polar opposite—faith. And I'm not simply talking about spiritual faith. I'm also talking about believing in yourself. Faith does require action, but the reward you'll receive by choosing to face your fears head-on is priceless. I know I'm preaching, but I don't want to censor myself out of fear of what people may think. That would totally contradict Steph's lesson. So, like her, I am following through!

Chapter Twelve
Coming Home

I first met Julie when she was the chair of a national working group we were both assigned to. Unfortunately, during that period one of our team members unexpectedly lost his life in a motor vehicle accident. To help the group move on, Julie held a sharing circle to allow for everybody to express how they were feeling or share some of our favorite memories of our late colleague and friend, a man named Barnaby. After that day, our group became closer and I became intrigued by the genuine kindness she showed towards us.

So I approached her to be a participant in this book—and I'm glad I did!

We met at a coffee shop later that same day. At first our conversation focused on the work we were doing, but eventually we transitioned into a discussion about her life and what she was thankful for.

I started off by asking her about her parents and she told me how they had both been unfairly saddled with abusive childhoods. To complicate their relationship even further, they were an interracial couple in a generation when the societally inept felt they had the right to pass judgment about their relationship. Between the pressure exerted on them through racism and their childhood traumas, eventually both of them began to struggle.

"That must have been tough on you growing up," I said. "Did you or your brother experience or witness their struggles?"

"No, not at all! It's probably because they had the courage to meet their challenges head-on when we were just babies. My childhood memories are happy, loving ones. I give them credit for that. They got help so we wouldn't have to go through what they did. I'm so proud of them. Actually, my first memories of my parents are of them teaching my brother and I how to be loving and kind. They also made sure we knew that it's important to express yourself when required, but they said it must always be done respectfully. They taught us that it's okay to be yourself and encouraged us to be who we were created to be. Looking back, I just needed to be me."

"Interesting that they both believed and knew there was a better way. What helped them to get back on track?"

"My mom was instrumental in seeking out help first. She chose therapy and spirituality to help address her issues. Mom's spirituality took her down a different path than Dad, and it definitely helped with her healing. She actually became a minister for a while. Dad soon followed, but he chose a more traditional route. It wasn't an easy journey for either of them, but it was one that they told me they needed to take. Dad has now been sober for over thirty-seven years. He is so strong. I look up to him for his leadership skills. He was also the chief of my community and was a drug and alcohol counselor. They've both worked so hard to get past those abusive experiences. They are such great people and role models for me and my brother."

Julie's obvious love and admiration for what her parents had worked through came out in every word she spoke. She may not have used the word thankful, but it was very clear that she was. She'd always had a very kind and gracious way about her—and based on what she shared with me, it was obvious that her parents were a big part of the reason why.

"It is very nice to see how thankful you are for your parents," I said. "Thank you for sharing that with me. Your early childhood sounds like it was a pretty good one. How were your high school years?"

"Pretty good. I had a few challenges here and there, some racism, but nothing too major. Thankfully, during those years Mom had decided to continue on with both her spirituality and therapy, so I often joined her on that journey as well. At the time, it was what I needed. I would say it helped me see the benefits of self-reflection and the honesty found within that process, but deep down I still felt a little lost and didn't really know why. No one would have known, because on the surface I appeared fine. I used my overachieving abilities to hide that. It worked for a while. I just did the things I was supposed to. I wasn't happy, though, because I wasn't being the real me."

"Do you mind if I ask you to talk a little more about what it was like trying to be someone other than yourself?"

"After I graduated, I went to university because it was the over-achieving thing to do. That's where my journey to find myself began. I started to learn for the first time about residential schools, which stirred me up on the inside. I began to feel like part of me was missing. I was Indigenous, but up until that point I had never fully searched out or embraced my culture. I didn't know how to handle what I was being taught. A professor told me that there was too much emotion in my paper on residential schools and that it wasn't 'good academic work.' I internalized this to mean that maybe I wasn't ready to examine First Nations history and thereby be a good advocate. The problem is that I believed her, because I didn't know myself yet. Internally, what she said didn't sit right with me. I knew my biggest betrayal was lying to myself, but I still did it. So on the surface I appeared fine because of my over-achieving, but internally I felt lost."

Julie had known her strategy to overachieve would eventually catch up with her. It wasn't who she was. She was only overachieving to survive her cultural identity struggle. She was smart and talented but didn't feel like she had the tools to address the issues in her heart. Instead of seeking counsel, she continued to try managing her internal battle. Ironically, the more she blindly chased after the myth of external happiness, the unhappier she became.

"I was academically successful," she continued. "I travelled to Ireland just because it was one of my childhood dreams. I got married. I was accepted into the PhD program at my dream school, Oxford University. But I was completely miserable. I started to ask myself, 'Is this what I really want? What would make me happy, truly happy? Who am I really? Why am I doing this?'"

In those self-reflective moments, she knew only one thing would help her reconcile with herself. She needed to return to her community to seek counsel. She needed to go home.

"I started to recognize that my happiness wouldn't be found until I found myself. So I did what others thought was crazy: I put Oxford on hold and returned home. At first it was hard. I regularly questioned my decision, but as time went on I began to understand why it had to be done. I'm sure people were judging me and my decision, but I didn't care. It was time to work on me."

"Were your parents upset that you dropped out of Oxford?" I asked. "What was their response to you suddenly coming home?"

"Not at all. They understood. They were super supportive. My parents are beautiful, amazing people. They let me work through what I needed to. I'm so thankful they did, because being home was super important in that process. I realize now that my decision to drop out of Oxford was an important step in setting me free. It was so important to my healing journey."

They say that everybody has a story, but what impressed me about Julie was her undeniable desire to become who she had been created to be, even if it cost her the so-called successes in life. Even more impressive was hearing her humble herself to the change process so she could become who she wanted to be.

Throughout our conversation, she expressed appreciation for those who helped her along the way. She's such a great example of what can happen when a person embraces the power of giving thanks.

"I'm so glad you agreed to share your story," I said. "I'm guessing that many things helped you work through becoming you. I'm sure there were a few up and down times during that process as well, but were there any defining moments you can share?"

"Multiple things got me back on track. My regular talks with an elder really helped. As far as a defining moment, I would say I had several, but the one that sticks out the most for me is when I was sitting in front of the lake back home. I was dragging my feet through the water, talking to Creator. I started asking him, 'What should I be doing? How can I reconcile who I am with myself?' It was during our talk that I got my answer. I didn't physically hear a voice, but I had a feeling come over me that was saying I needed to come home to myself."

"What did you do?"

"Right after that, I started putting a real effort into becoming me. I did a lot of self-reflection. I evaluated my life in all areas to see what did or didn't align with the real me. That helped me to abandon who I was pretending to be. It allowed me to reconnect with my culture, which used to be foreign to me. Since that day, I have never looked back."

"Your courage and resolve to make such an important decision is really admirable!" I said encouragingly. "Listening to you, it seems that the teachings your parents spoke and modeled were also a significant part of your success. Would you agree?"

"Yes. My parents and their teachings continue to guide me throughout my life. It took a while to sink in, but I realized there are more important things in life. It's more important to do good and to do good work. It's about being aligned and using your gifts with the time we have here. I now wake up asking myself three probing questions. I've actually written them on my wall so they are the first things I see when I get up in the morning."

"What did you write?"

"The first one asks Creator, 'What would you have me do today?' The second is 'Creator, where would you have me go?' And the third is 'Creator, what would you have me say?' They help me start my day in a good way, and I'm so thankful that I understand my purpose now. So grateful!"

"It sounds to me like you have found your home, figuratively and literally. I love your story of self-reconciliation. Thank you for sharing. Can I ask a few last questions? Of all your experiences to date, what are you most thankful for, and how has being thankful helped you with that journey?"

"That's easy. I'm definitely thankful for my perspective shift and for self-reflection. For my parents, my community, and the Creator for guiding me home. I'm thankful that I got so low, because it enabled me to surrender and come home. I am thankful for my late friend and colleague Barnaby, for encouraging me to play my drum with confidence. I'm thankful for what a gift life is! I'm thankful for what I get to do day in and day out. Why am I thankful? It helps me remember who I am and who I need to be."

Social norms shouldn't be allowed to define who you really are. Coming home is more than a deep thought; it's an important journey with yourself so that you can be who you were created to be.

Chapter Thirteen
My Place in this World

I grew up in a small town where everybody knew everybody. Bev lived across the street from me in my high school years and was a friend of the family I boarded with. One day, she posted about her son and it caused something to stir up inside me.

In fact, it was so touching that I decided to reach out to her to see if she would be willing to share her story for the thankfulness project. And to my delight, she said yes.

"Thanks for agreeing to meet with me and to be part of my book, Bev," I began. "I know you've shared with others that November 17, 1996 is a day you will never forget. If it's okay with you, could you walk me through that life-changing experience?"

"Yes, I'm in a good place now. So if it helps someone else find their way, I'm all for it. I remember that day like it was yesterday. I was lying in my bed going through what I needed to do for the day. Normally I would have gotten up right away and headed straight to the kitchen, but because I was almost full-term, let's just say I needed to make a bit more of an effort to get to my feet."

The multiple processes women must go through to bring life into this world has always amazed me—from dealing with the awkward pregnancy dance to the endless unanswered questions hovering on the periphery of their thoughts, to everything else that goes along with having a child. God definitely chose the right gender to deliver such a precious gift.

"Did you always want children?" I asked.

"To be honest, there was a point in my life when I didn't want to have kids. I'm not sure if you know this, but both of my parents were alcoholics. It was tough growing up in that environment. I never felt supported. I was bullied, and for the longest time I allowed all of that unhealthy s#!t I experienced to control my life."

It's hard enough to be a child in a sometimes unfriendly world, but having to do it on your own because "the bottle" has become the center of your parents' addictive worlds is a path no child should have to start out on.

"I didn't know that," I said. "Sorry that was your experience. I'm sure their addiction made it quite tough on you growing up. What would you say helped you along the way to get to the healthier place you are at today?"

"I'm definitely in a much better place but I would say I am still a work in progress, and I realize now that there's nothing wrong with that—as long as I keep making improvements. Lots of small things helped me, but probably one of the most definitive life events which contributed to my healing process is my son. It all started with him."

The revelation in those two statements, for me, was the word *making*. It gets to the idea of undergoing the long, slow process of breaking through pain. Facing our worst nightmares is among the hardest processes a person will ever go through, but it often ends up being among the most rewarding.

"Would you be able to walk me through what you mean when you say your son started you off on your healing?"

"Ever since we lost Adam, my husband's and my goal has been to help someone else if we can," Bev said. "I'm okay to do that now. Before I share about the morning of that day, and all the rest, I have to be honest: none of this has been easy. It's been a long road for me and my family and I've had to work through a lot to get to this stage. But I'm so glad I did. I just needed to say that. Now, the morning of, I was having my coffee when I started feeling sharp, tightening, stabbing pains in my tummy. The best way I can describe it is that it felt like a strong bear hug. At first I thought this was nothing more than normal pregnancy pains, but they persisted and got quite intense."

At home by herself, Bev entered into a mental discussion with herself about what to do next. It was her first pregnancy and she wasn't exactly sure if these sensations meant she was in labor, or if it was even an issue at all.

However, as the morning went on, the intensity and frequency of her pains became more than she could bear. So she decided to walk over to her in-laws' home to get a second opinion.

By the time she got there, she could no longer pretend she wasn't in pain.

"I remember walking through their door and needing to sit down," she said. "I was in so much pain. My father-in-law straight out asked me if I was okay. I remember emphatically saying, "*No*, I am not okay. I think I need to go to the hospital. Something doesn't feel right… I think I'm in labor."

So instead of taking the wait-and-see approach, together she and her family made the hour-long trek to the hospital. She said that the minutes felt like hours and she felt increasingly uncomfortable during the drive.

"My anxiety levels were through the roof," she said. "I wasn't feeling quite right, and for some reason I couldn't shake the thought that maybe something was wrong."

Fortunately, the winter road conditions held up and they were able to make it to the hospital in good time. Upon arrival she was quickly processed at emergency and immediately taken to the maternity floor.

"I remember putting my gown on and saying to myself or my husband, not sure which, 'Why does my door have a blue butterfly on it?' I'm sure the other doors didn't."

Sadly, the answer to that question came several minutes later when she was informed that her baby would bypass its time on earth to become an angel in heaven.

As you can imagine, her whole world crashed in on her.

"When they told me, I went numb," she said. "I couldn't get any words to come out of my mouth, but on the inside I was screaming, 'Why me? Why my baby? I did everything by the book!' I had felt so alive and healthy during my pregnancy. How the hell had this happened?"

The unbelievable pain that accompanied the loss of her first child was further compounded when she learned that, for medical reasons, her best option would be to carry him for an additional eleven days.

"I can't even imagine processing that memory and what you went through," I said. "You are one strong woman! How did you get through the eleven days and beyond? I'm not trying to intrude, so please know that if you don't want to answer, I fully understand and respect that."

"It's an important question," she said. "I wouldn't be here to talk if I wasn't ready to share this part of me. I'm really hopeful that in my sharing, it helps someone else who may have lost a child or had a similar experience to mine. Just so you know, in my answer you may get way more than you need, but talking about it is a sort of therapy for me."

"I understand. Take your time."

"In those eleven days, I tried my very best to keep things as normal as possible! We found out on a Wednesday evening. Thursday, I can't even recall what I did. Friday, I met with the obstetrician and found out that they definitely were not going to induce me. I just had to wait until I went into labor, so I did anything I could to occupy my brain. I just stayed busy, as I wasn't ready to fully face it yet. I played solitaire, baked, cleaned, and went for walks and to the doctors' appointments. I actually had to sit with all the other pregnant ladies in the waiting room and answer the 'when are you due?' question more times than I care to remember. All I know is that I couldn't have made it if I hadn't kept my family and friends close. I processed my loss one day at a time and as best I could! I won't say I didn't cry a lot or question our higher power a hundred times a day, because I did. I may have thrown a few objects out of pure frustration as well! The real tears came after I gave birth. I can still hear the nurse saying, 'Okay, Bev, time to push. And again, and again. That's it, my dear. Your baby boy is delivered.' He was seven pounds, eight ounces, twenty-four inches long, with dark hair, all ten fingers, all ten toes, a button nose, chubby cheeks that had started to peel, sweet hands, sweet everything… just no breath… no cry… no heartbeat. Silence. The worst silence I've ever heard."

Adam Rousson quietly entered the world at 6:47 p.m. on Sunday, November 17, 1996. Today and every day, Bev says she rests a little easier knowing that their baby boy is in heaven alongside some of the best people she knows. She has also said that she's comforted in knowing that one day they will meet again.

"Adam is always right here in my heart," she said. "He was my first born, breathless but still my first. He made me a mother. He made me stronger. He helped me to heal some old wounds, and he helped me find my place in this world."

"Thanks for sharing that with me, Bev. I know it must have been difficult for you to relive those heartbreaking memories. I know it's deeply personal information and I want you to know that writing your story is not something I take lightly."

"Like I said, Derek, it's all good. It's therapeutic. What else would you like to know? I'll give you whatever I can if it helps someone else."

As we continued to talk, she told me that her choice to find goodness in the midst of such a dark time in her life didn't happen immediately. She reached out for help to a multitude of resources that had been presented to her and eventually found a space where she felt safe.

"At the time, I needed someone who would just listen to me and maybe share with me some of the pain they had suffered and what had helped them. I was introduced to a group for people who had lost children from miscarriage to murder. I immediately knew that this was where I needed to be at that time in my life. I even met a young lady my own age with a similar story to mine. It was one of the first times I really felt like I wasn't alone in this."

Fast-forward five months and she was sharing her story with a room of about sixty people at a national conference.

"Even though I was talking about the most painful experience in my life, I was very happy. Because that experience helped me and I got to experience firsthand how what I shared helped others. Two young moms in this group cried with me after I shared and they both opened up about their crazy thoughts and feelings. I was able to assure them that they weren't crazy. I totally understood, because I had felt the same way in the beginning."

It goes without saying that Bev is an incredible woman and example of perseverance. Granted, the process of finding the good in her situation wasn't her first instinct, nor was it easy, but she would be the first to attest that it's one of the best things she did to move forward with her life.

"Bev, thank you so much for being a part of this book, and thank you for your willingness to share so much of your deeply personal story. I would like to close with a few last questions on thankfulness, if you don't mind. In all that you've been through, good and not-so-good, how has being thankful helped you and what are you most thankful for?"

"That is a really good question, but if it's okay, I would like to think about my response and get back to you. Would that be okay?"

"Absolutely! Whenever you're ready, send it, and I'll add it in."

Several days later, I received her response. What an amazing perspective! What an incredible testimony on thankfulness.

> After some very personal moments of self-reflection, I am thankful for the strength I got from being forced to deal with the childhood/teenage issues I had pushed away and refused to deal with. It took a horrible unbearable situation like losing our baby to help pull myself up out of a self-hating existence and to realize that I wasn't the ugly, nasty person I had been led to believe I was.
>
> I am completely thankful for our three girls, and that because I worked through our family's loss I am able to help them (in a much healthier way) to deal with the everyday issues of growing up, like being teased or being made fun of. I'm thankful I have been able to provide some help to my daughters

in an effective, loving way because I can relate to how they feel when those types of things happen.

I am now more willing to tell my daughters about my experiences and what I have learned. Basically, I have taken a broken person and slowly put her back together, day by day turning her back into the wonderful, loving person she truly is! I truly believe that my place in this world is helping others find their inner beauty and letting it shine regardless of what anyone tells them or what they believe about themselves. I am forever thankful for the gift of my son and what he has given me!

I love you, Adam—always and forever. Love, Mom.

Wow. What a perspective. I couldn't imagine the pain she experienced, but being able to find the good despite the darkness speaks volumes to the warrior woman she is. We are all created uniquely, and it's in those differences that we can all be totally blessed. We all have a purpose and a place in this world. No matter what anyone ever tells you, *never* believe any different!

Chapter Fourteen
No Silver Bullet

"My hope is that in sharing my struggle, someone might be encouraged to turn over a new page in their life, to fight another day and take one more step forward, even if they feel they've just taken three steps back. After all, there is hope and I want them to know that they are not alone." Janice paused. "Okay, enough preamble. Let's get into it. I've struggled with mental health issues."

What a brave statement to put out into the universe. I've known Janice and her husband TJ for more than fifteen years. Ever since reading her blog post first talking about these issues, I've been a fan of how she expresses herself. So when I started doing interviews for this book, I knew I had to ask her to be part of it.

"I'm not going to lie," she said. "When you first contacted me, I was a little nervous about what level of detail you needed, but after some self-reflection, I realized that some of the revelations that have helped me the most have come through the stories of others. So after talking with TJ, I thought, *I'm doing this!* I hope others will be able to relate to it."

Whether people want to admit it or not, the increased demands and societal stress being imposed on our lives has created significant challenges to living a thankful life. The days of mental health being dismissed or inaccurately stigmatized are slowly reversing because people like Janice are being brave enough to share their journeys.

"I'm sure many people will gain a whole new way of looking at and thinking about mental health because of your story," I said. "Can you tell me a bit about growing up and your family life?"

"I came from a loving home. I guess that's why I never wanted to talk with anyone about my depression struggles. I was concerned people would think I had no reason to be depressed."

"That must have been emotionally draining for you."

"Yes, it was. When I had my worst bouts of depression, it felt like I had a gaping wound that no one else could see. I was in so much pain, but I convinced myself that if I shared my struggles I would be seen as flawed and be treated differently. So I pretended everything was fine. I said nothing. I was afraid people would look at me like I was talking about the warts on my feet. It's just not something we talk about."

"How were you able to hide it so well?"

"You put on your mask and pretend life is awesome. If someone asked me how I was doing, I would smile and say, 'I'm great, how are you?'"

Admitting to others that she was struggling wasn't the cultural norm at that time in her life, and in many ways it still isn't fully embraced today. We live in a generation of social media users who can skillfully assemble and seduce us into believing people are living picture perfect lives. If we aren't careful, we begin to believe everybody else has it all together. That isn't the truth!

"Janice, prior to calling you I reflected back on some of the times we got together with your family and I just remember seeing you as the quiet happy person."

"I am a quiet person, and I did have good days," she said. "There were also some stretches of time when I felt okay, but inevitably they always seemed to be short-lived. In those moments you're talking about, I may have been having a good day. But more than likely, I was acting, or I was willing myself through those moments."

"What do you mean, you were willing yourself? Can you explain that a little more for me?"

"Sure. By willing myself, I mean I would just psych myself up for the social interactions. I may have appeared to have it all together, but what people didn't see was how I emotionally crashed afterwards. All of the faking and willing myself into action was burning me out. I was becoming increasingly frustrated with life. I began to feel like I was literally PMSing fifteen to twenty days each month. My life became too much to manage, so I withdrew more and more from friends, my family, and the ones closest to me. I started to spend a lot of time alone and I truly felt like they were better off if I wasn't around them."

"That sounds like it was a pretty tough time in your life. How did you find your way out of that dark and lonely place?"

"I just remember waking up one day and saying to myself enough was enough. I was tired of feeling so emotionally exhausted and I didn't want to live that way anymore, so I confided my struggles to one of my closest friends. She already knew I struggled, but not the full story. Acknowledging my real struggle was a defining moment for me because she was able to help me see that I'm not flawed and that maybe I hadn't fully embraced all the options available to me."

"What did she say that helped you"

"She knew that one of the options I avoided, because of the stigma associated with it, was taking a pill," Janice said. "She was able to help me realize that all kinds of people take medication to help them with physical health issues without any stigma, so why should it be any different with mental health issues? Why is someone who needs an antidepressant viewed as weak when someone who needs insulin for diabetes isn't? She convinced me that there was absolutely nothing wrong with exploring that option. Health is health!"

I think it's fair to say that everybody could use the support and guidance Janice received from her friend in her moment of need, especially when it comes to the challenges associated with mental health. Often, our eventual breakthroughs come as a direct result of sharing with a trusted friend. We all need to get back to personal interactions.

"Thanks for being so honest about your times of struggle," I said. "I'm guessing that what you just shared with me helped you to improve your mental health and to write your blog post about why you were going on meds."

"Yes, it did help me to improve my mental health, and I was eventually able to get off all medication with the help of amino acid therapy and a functional medicine approach, which I'm completely thankful for. But at the time, the meds did help me regain some normalcy in my life. They gave me the ability to process my thoughts with more clarity. But honestly, on top of the meds, I couldn't have done it without the support of my friends and family, and my husband. If it weren't for TJ stepping up in every instance, I'm not sure if I would be in the spot I am today. He did so much for me and the family during those not-so-good times. He never complained. He just one hundred percent supported me. I never felt judged by him. He encouraged me to talk about it and to put my story out there. I was so nervous, but his support got me through it. He truly has shown unconditional love to me in the highs and lows, right from the day we got married. I couldn't have done it without him."

What an incredibly uplifting and honest response. Yes, the meds helped guide her to a new way of thinking, but I was inspired to hear her acknowledgement that her spouse supported her so fully. There may be no silver bullets, but her account of what TJ did for her is definitely golden!

"Thank you for sharing your wellness journey with me," I said. "It's definitely a story that needs to be told. If you could pass on some advice to other women about that time in your life, what would it be?"

"For me, it would be to not let fear ruin your life. Use wisdom. Don't allow the unfair stigma associated with mental health stop you from reaching out or from accessing the strategies and resources you need if you find yourself struggling."

We all need systems and strategies to make it through the daily grind. Especially in this culture where we're never allowed to turn our brains off, Janice is right that we should use wisdom.

"Before I let you go, I have two final questions for you. What would you say you are most thankful for, and how has being thankful helped you get to where you are today?"

"Good questions! I'm thankful for the people who supported me on this journey. I'm also thankful that I'm now able to help and support others who are struggling in the same ways I did. You know, something I didn't expect, but which I'm really thankful for, is that I get to see and feel what it's like to help loved ones going through this. It can be really tough to walk alongside someone who's battling depression, but I'm grateful I get to be that person. It makes me even more thankful for my support system and the patience they've all shown me, including my mom, who always supported me and encouraged me to get help—long before I finally did. TJ, my husband, is amazing. I'm so thankful I have him. I am especially thankful for God being with me along the way. I'm thankful that I am much better at knowing what to do if depression rises up from time to time. When emotionally abusive thoughts pop into my mind, I am way better at kicking them to the curb where they belong. They no longer control me.

"I think it's important for people to know that you don't one day arrive at a perfect thought life. There will always be peaks and valleys, but because of all the work I've done and the physical health changes I have made, that journey is no longer an uphill battle. I'm so grateful for that! It's been a journey, and being thankful continues to help me each day. Without gratitude, I wouldn't be in the spot I am today."

There is no silver bullet when it comes to mental health. What works for one may not necessarily work for another. It's incredibly important for people to know and understand that. Never stop believing, never stop searching, and never be afraid to reach out.

Chapter Fifteen
Back to Basics

I was blessed to mentor Kyra as a summer student a few years ago. During our time together, she shared with me that at a young age she endured the pain of losing her boyfriend to a drunk driver and experienced situational racism simply because of the color of her skin.

Yet the moment I came into contact with her, I immediately felt her zest for life. It was as if she had discovered that the world was her oyster and no person, event, or thing could stop her from enjoying or pursuing the gift of life. She now spends literally every minute of every day yearning to explore God's magnificent creation, and I wanted to know more about how she cultivated this passion.

"Hey Kyra! Thanks for being part of this. Let's start with your early childhood years. Tell me about them, about growing up. Where did you live? Where did you go to school? What was high school like?"

"In elementary school, I had no major problems. It was pretty normal. I lived with both of my parents in two separate homes. They separated when I was one, so that was all I knew. I wasn't angry about their divorce. I didn't know any different. They found a way to get along.

They made it work. I always felt loved by both my mom and my dad. I grew up in Winnipeg and all my schooling was there. I have pretty good memories. Teenage years! They were typical. I was one of the only First Nations kids in my school. I experienced some negative things in my school, but after I got to travel to New York for a school trip I realized that my struggles actually weren't that big."

I was struck by how self-reflective she was. Rarely have I heard people in their early twenties talk about their past as a learning moment.

"You said your high school trip helped you realize that the things you thought were big issues actually weren't that big after all. What did you mean by that?"

"When I was fifteen, I was selected to go to New York City to represent my school as part of a United Nations opportunity. When you're in high school, you tend to believe your life is only within four walls. You can't see beyond your circumstances. That experience made me realize that school is such a small part of life and our issues in Canada aren't that big. The world is so much more than that. It changed my perspective. It expanded my worldwide perspective. It helped me to realize that my problems at home were minor. It made me want to see the world. It made me thankful for what I have. It made me realize that there was so much more to life."

Even though we were doing the interview via telephone, I felt her truth through every word. I pointed out to her that I noticed her voice grew excited when she talked about wanting to see the world.

"I do! When I was eighteen, I was in Greece and it hit me that I really loved to travel and meet people. I decided then that even though it may seem strange to other people, I was going to travel the world on my own. It makes me happy, but it also keeps me grounded. When I went to South Africa, I saw there was very little government support and the poverty was widespread, but to witness the resilience of the people was inspiring. It made me appreciate that Canada isn't perfect, but I do have support and it is pretty good. I have been to over forty countries, from Southeast Asia to Columbia. Every trip makes me realize how fortunate I am. I just love it! I plan on taking a one-year leave of absence from work to live abroad and travel. I can't wait."

"You've obviously found your passion—and you're so young! How do you afford to do it?"

She laughed. "It's simple. I make it a priority."

There I was, sitting on my couch, unexpectedly receiving the best advice from someone I had once mentored. Over the years, Kyra and I had remained good friends—but until that moment, I hadn't realized she was also mentoring me. A valuable lesson indeed!

"Look who's life-coaching now, Kyra! Tell me how you make it a priority."

"Nothing is easy. You need to put a plan in place and work hard at it. You have to put the work into it. Growing up, we didn't have a lot of money and my parents taught me to work hard and with purpose if you wanted something."

As a parent, you often wonder if you've done right by your children. You ask yourself whether you've given them enough tools to thrive in this sometimes challenging world. I think it's safe to say that Kyra's parents have done that and then some.

"Kyra, you never cease to amaze me," I said. "Sounds like you're on your way to figuring life out. Good for you! If you don't mind, I would like to ask you a few personal questions on the loss of your boyfriend. Don't feel like you have to, but I'm just wondering if you could share how you got through that."

"Yes, I'm ready to share that. He was killed by a drunk driver. We were planning on travelling together, and then I got a call. It hurt, and getting through it wasn't easy, but I can honestly say that his passing has taught me so much. I chose to focus on being grateful for the lessons he taught me. I learned a lot about myself, other people, time, my values, and how short life is! We all get in a car and assume we will get home safe and sound. I learned that isn't always true. It sparked something in me. I was no longer willing to let fear control what I wanted in life. It taught me to be kind and appreciate others, because you never know when you may lose someone. He had called me that very morning before he passed, and that is a moment I will cherish forever."

Did I mention that Kyra is only in her twenties? What a perspective to have. Someone once said, "If you focus on the hurt, you will continue to suffer. But if you focus on the lesson, you will continue to grow." From my perspective, Kyra is a true example of that. She's always looking for a way to become a better person, internally and externally, because she has chosen to find the good.

"Thank you for that, Kyra. From all of your life experiences to date, how has being thankful helped you and what are you most thankful for?"

"Love! It's all about love. Love can conquer all. We need to be grateful for the gifts we have, including our health and our jobs. We must not take life for granted. When you see people living in shipping containers with no food, it puts everything back into perspective. We need to get back to the basics. I used to care so much about what people thought of me, but I realized at a young age that it doesn't really matter. I now live by a saying: 'It's none of my business what others think of me.'

"I've learned that love is all we need, and it's what drives us forward in life. I'm not going to take life for granted. I'm going to follow my dreams and pursue my passions, which right now are traveling and living abroad. I'm all about challenging my comfort zone too. I don't want to be afraid or governed by fear. It's important to me to not let fear get in the way of accomplishing my goals and dreams, and that includes any type of fear: fear of the unknown, fear of rejection, fear of failure. I believe that all lessons, the good and the difficult, are teachable moments and an opportunity to reflect and grow as a person. I'm thankful that I realized this now and that I can forge a path that is full of love and light.

"I'm also guided by my faith. It's an important aspect for me. I walk forth with my ancestors and guardian angels surrounding me, the love and support of my family and the presence of God guiding me. I always ensure that I give thanks to the Creator for the blessings I have. My faith helps me remain humble and grounded as I navigate this amazing journey called life."

We truly can get back to basics if we're willing to incorporate thankfulness into our daily living. It won't solve all your challenges, but it certainly will assist you in enjoying and appreciating the gift of life.

Chapter Sixteen
Giving Back

As I reached over and turned my alarm clock off, a small smile formed on my face. Not because I loved mornings, but because I was starting to realize how the Thankfulness Project was impacting me in ways I had never expected. Who would have thought waking up and being alive would have been something to be thankful for? Who would have thought that my getting-up-on-the-wrong-side-of-the-bed syndrome could be partially cured by a concentrated daily focus on being thankful? Who would have thought that a 7:00 a.m. interview call would be something I looked forward to all week?

I'm so thankful that all these questions migrated into my new way of thinking. Either way, I was about to speak with Alyssa, another great example of someone who walks the walk and talks the talk when it comes to thankfulness.

"Thanks for making space in your day to do this, Alyssa. I know you have another appointment this morning, so I'll jump right into the interview."

"Thank you for getting up so early! I was hoping I could make a later time work, but I have a volunteer training session with Homeless

Connect Toronto today. That's why I suggested such an early start time."

Her apology for squeezing me in gave me even more confirmation that she was who I perceived her to be. I had anticipated that our conversation would push me to think differently, but I hadn't expected the learning to happen so quickly.

"That's really impressive," I said. "Volunteering with the homeless isn't something people often choose to do on the weekend, especially a Saturday morning. Can you tell me a little bit more about Homeless Connect and how you ended up volunteering with them?"

"I was looking to give back in an area I hadn't before. I was very aware of homelessness in my city, but I hadn't known what I could actually do to address it. A friend of mine introduced me to Homeless Connect Toronto, which serves as an annual one-stop shop for people experiencing homelessness. All the essential services are under one roof to help people find their way back onto their feet. Each person has a story, as we all do. In the beginning, it was a complete eye-opening experience for me. I've learned so much about homelessness and its impacts. This experience has caused me to pause and listen… and it keeps me grounded. It helps to bring me back to my center."

"When you say it brings you back to center, can you expand on that a little? Do you mean it helps you to be more thankful?"

"Exactly. It makes me recognize that there is so much to be grateful for."

It was interesting to hear Alyssa share about how her experience had impacted her life, because the exact same experience had started me on this journey.

"Very cool! Interesting how giving back works, isn't it? Have you always volunteered? Why do you do it?"

"Honestly, I believe part of why I volunteer is because I witnessed my parents doing it day in and day out. From as early as I can remember, my parents have always put others first. It was what they did, and continue to still do, on a daily basis. It was indirect training, I suppose. I never wanted to admit to it as a child, but as an adult I'm so thankful they taught me to be grateful and help others. They were great role models and I am thankful for that."

Her response was refreshing and humbling. Refreshing because she gave credit to her parents for modeling the philosophy that it's better to serve others than to be served, and humbling because she was putting those life lessons into action by giving back while expecting nothing in return.

"Sounds like you had great parents," I said.

"They raised us well and I always knew I was loved and supported. I had a really happy upbringing. We lived in the suburbs and had all we needed. Probably my biggest challenge was that my parents were in the public eye and I had to deal with the pressure associated with that. Other than that, no complaints!"

As she told me about her childhood and her parents giving back, I gained a better understanding of why she emitted the thankfulness vibe.

"You said that part of your desire to help others comes from your upbringing," I continued. "What else has influenced you?"

"There are a couple of moments of thankfulness that stand out for me. One of them was as an adult and the other was in my high school years. I think it was grade ten that social causes and issues started to appear on my radar, after returning to Toronto from a youth group trip to northern Alberta. I became fast friends with a girl my age who lived on the reserve we visited. We kept in touch for years and shared many of the same ambitions, but she faced many more barriers to those ambitions than I ever did, simply because of where she lived. I realized how fortunate I was in the many invisible supports that surrounded me. I realized then that I had the privilege of opportunity while many others my own age were in need of just one. It bothered me. I wanted to give back somehow. So when I went to school to get my education degree, I requested that my teaching placement be on a First Nation. That placement opened my eyes up to more of the difficulties my friend must have faced, and I'm thankful that it continues to influence my work today. It was an Aha! moment for sure."

"Those are some wise words and reflections. Can you tell me more about that placement and Aha! moment you experienced?"

"It came while I was doing my teaching practicum," Alyssa said. "The community had two sudden deaths within two weeks and then were flooded out at the same time. I hadn't imagined anything like that until I experienced it for myself. I wouldn't have ever understood what some communities have to regularly deal with. That experience really made me want to do more and be better."

Many of us go through life not making changes in our lives when we learn new information. Not Alyssa. After her experience on the reserve, she had the first of many gut, head, and heart checks. She began asking questions like, *What can I do to help? How can I show I care?* After some self-reflection, she promised herself that she would always endeavor to do more and be better.

"Volunteering is all about perspective," she said. "For me, volunteering helps me to do my work better. I need those reminders that we're all just people. Imagine if we all united to help one another and put in a little bit of care each day. The world would definitely be a much better place. It's humbling to be part of something bigger than yourself. I really just want to continue to work in the most impactful way."

My brief chat with Alyssa stirred something in me in terms of helping others. It also made me want to start finding ways to give back.

"I've really enjoyed our talk this morning," I said. "You said you would help out in any way you can, and believe me you have. I notice that it's getting close to the end of the time you have available, I would like to ask my final two questions. The first is, what are you most thankful for? And the second is, how has thankfulness helped you throughout your life?"

"When I think of thankfulness, I'm brought back to Shawn Anchor's TED Talk on happiness. He explained that when you raise your level of positivity in the present, you are happier and your brain actually performs better in all aspects. A friend and I watched the talk and wanted to practice being positive in the present by writing down three things we were thankful for on a daily basis. We challenged each other to a one-month commitment and ended up writing to each other for an entire year. With my friend being in Washington DC, and myself in Toronto, we wrote hundreds of these to each other. Doing this made me pause every night to reflect on what good had taken place, and soon I was pausing midday to acknowledge things that had brought me joy. Whether it was experiencing a significant event or a small act of kindness, writing down my 'thankfuls' made me happier, and being happier allowed me to remain motivated in being purposeful. I'm most thankful to have learned how to practice gratefulness, and I hope I never stop working at it."

Volunteering and giving back truly do help us create a new perspective, especially when it's done with a thankful heart. As Alyssa said, "Imagine if we all united to help one another and put in a little bit of care each day. The world would definitely be a much better place."

Chapter Seventeen
Good Vibrations

Brenna and I had been friends for several years, and whenever I had the chance to interact with her I was inspired by her glass-half-full perspective, especially when it came to the challenges of life. I often wondered what her story was and how she managed to keep such a positive outlook on situations.

Thankfully, she agreed to share some of the why and how with me.

Brenna's parents divorced when she was just four years old. It was a day she has never forgotten.

"I was sitting on our grey couch in the living room when my mom and dad both came in," she told me. "They both had sad looks on their faces and my mom looked like she had been crying. I knew something wasn't right. We used to have this old scratchy blue blanket in there and I pulled it over my head. I guess I thought it would stop what was about to come. My heart was racing. I was crying, and then they told me they were getting a divorce. I was devastated by the loss of my family. It was tough. It created a belief in me that nothing lasts forever."

Like all kids, Brenna just wanted the family life she had come to love and enjoy. Unfortunately, she found herself unwillingly in the process of building a new normal. At the age of four, nothing could have prepared her for that.

"It just isn't the same living in two separate homes. My parents tried to do their best, but there often weren't those teachable moments that come from a two-parent relationship. They also both moved on to other relationships, and that created a whole other challenge for me. I felt like I needed to act or live in a certain way so I didn't disappoint either of my parents. It created an anxiety in me that I didn't have before. I didn't fully get where or how I fit into their relationship and all the stuff that goes with that. I really struggled with that, especially in my teenage years."

Struggling to find her way in a world she knew nothing about, she kept her insecurities to herself and simply became what her environment dictated to her.

Lost and confused, she turned to a trusted friend to confide in about how she was feeling on the inside. She says his caring ear was one of her saving graces.

"Thankfully, I had my best friend. I used to tell him everything. Actually, we used to tell each other everything. I'm so glad I had him to talk to back then."

"Is he still your best friend?" I asked. "Are you still in touch with him?"

"He ended up moving away. That really sucked, because he was someone I trusted. I knew he had my back and that I could confide in him. I never really had a best friend like him after that. I made and lost friends along the way, but none that I truly believed would be there for me! I have them now, of course, but I'm in my thirties!"

We all have times when a true and trusted friend is worth their weight in gold, someone you can share with or vent to in a nonjudgmental environment. Unfortunately, the loss of that opportunity for Brenna caused her to push her emotions aside and go back into her protective shell.

"Why do you think it was so hard to find another friend like you had in your youth?"

"You learn quickly that some people don't always believe you when they can't physically see your pain," she said. "You just bury what you're going through to cope. So I just wore a mask forever. At the time, it was all I knew how to do."

"What allowed you to quit wearing a mask?"

"I decided to search out resources that were available to me. I found a few support groups that helped, as they validated what I was going through and helped me express myself a little better. I also became friends with a woman who encouraged me to be authentically me. She taught me not to apologize for being myself. She helped me see that I didn't need to pretend to be something I wasn't. It was okay if I wasn't what others thought I should be. After that, I started telling myself, 'You do count.' Even today, when my emotions ramp up and take over for a bit, I embrace them only for a moment and then, instead of letting them consume my thoughts, I find a way to work through them quickly and move on. I'm thankful for my experiences with the support groups and my friend who encouraged me. Both helped me grow in a good way."

Brenna was able to realize that there are places to seek counsel when we're struggling emotionally. And because of her self-reflective efforts and the supports she received from others, she now has a process in place that allows her to get herself back on track when the need arises.

"Thanks for sharing the different things that have worked for you. Maybe it will inspire someone else to do the same," I said. "I was wondering, can we go back to your childhood best friend for a second? I forgot to ask: did you ever get the chance to thank him or reconnect?"

"We did get to reconnect for a bit, but he ended up taking his own life. That is something I will never forget. He was having some personal identity issues. I guess the stress from it all became too much and he couldn't cope. I never knew it was that bad for him. I really do miss him and our conversations. Losing him made me recognize that making an effort and staying in contact with people you value is super important. So now, no matter the distance, I make the effort with my friends that are important to me."

An elder once told me that life is all about relationships. It took me years to fully understand the breadth and depth of that statement, but Brenna's reflection brought it back to life for me. It truly is so important to make sure that we support and stay in touch with those to whom we are closest.

"It isn't always easy finding good in not-so-good situations, but it's kind of cool to see how you've used those experiences to help you work through some tougher life issues," I said. "Is there anything else you care to share that has impacted you in a good way?"

"Interesting that you ask that question, because last night I was thinking back to the things in my life that helped me become me. My move to Victoria after graduation was certainly one of them. That was one of the best decisions of my life."

"How so?"

"For the first time, I actually felt like it was okay to be myself. I felt free. No one was defining who I should or shouldn't be. I started looking for the good in everything. I realized that my experiences weren't necessarily the norm. If I wanted a healthy family dynamic, I could choose to have that… and if I truly wanted something, I should go after it. When I returned home, I had a newfound confidence. It was the best experience. I'm so thankful for that."

It was interesting to see how she was able to transport her thought process back in time to moments that provided her with tangible feelings of gratitude. Fascinated by witnessing firsthand her emotional payback from being thankful, I made a mental note to try finding it myself later.

"Your story is thankfulness in action," I said. "I actually felt a little bit of what you experienced because of how you shared it. I felt like I was right there with you. I truly am enjoying talking with you. Do you have time for a few more questions?"

"Not sure I have much more to share, but ask away."

"We've talked about your youth and how you found your way back to yourself in adulthood. What's next for you?"

"Marriage maybe. I have a great guy. He is my partner in crime, my love, my life… but children, probably not. I don't share this much, but a few years ago I was diagnosed with an auto immune disorder called endometriosis. I had to have emergency surgery and it left a nasty scar. I was told that I had virtually no hope of being able to have children naturally."

There I sat, trying to pull my size-nine foot out of my mouth. I had no idea she was suffering like she was. Even worse, I had no idea what endometriosis was.

"Sorry, Brenna. I would have never known. To be honest, I don't know what endometrioses is."

"That's okay. Most people don't know about it. It's when the tissue that makes up the uterine lining—in other words, the womb—is present on other organs in the body. It causes me severe pelvic and abdominal pain, among other things. My insides freak out with certain foods, which really sucks as I'm such a foodie. My weight is an endless struggle. My hormones are generally out of whack due to this disease. I've had two laparoscopies because of it and I have been medically induced into menopause, but this isn't going to stop me from living my life. I will find a way through it. I will continue to think positively and go after what I want. I will move forward to create what I'm passionate about. I will keep looking for the good vibrations in my life."

"Your story is exactly the type I wanted to capture. I wanted a real person. You are definitely that! There's so much good in what you have shared. What you told me this evening is going to be someone's hope, healing, or breakthrough."

"Really?" she said. "Thanks. My story seems kind of boring. Are you sure you're getting what you wanted?"

"In no way is your story boring. The way you handle life is pretty amazing, if you ask me. So thank you for participating! I do have one last question for you, though, if that's okay? It's something I'm asking all the women I've interviewed. What are you most thankful for? And how would you say that being thankful has helped you up to this point in your life?"

"Honestly, I'm most thankful for having recognized that the power to live and be happy is within me. I get to control my environment and live the way I want to live. Humans are made to pass on love, and my goal is to continually do that. Struggles are a part of life. Choosing to live is up to each of us, and I'm thankful I have that opportunity. As for thankfulness, it has grounded me. There is so much more in life to look at than the not-so-goods. It has helped root me in the awareness that there will be good times that outshine the bad ones, even when they come around less often. Thankfulness must be practiced. Otherwise it is fleeting!"

Brenna is correct. Being true to oneself requires reflection and the recognition that the power to live and be happy is within us all. Becoming who you truly are is a process, not an end state. So embrace the journey and be thankful while doing it.

Chapter Eighteen
Waffle Breakfast Roll Call

As we sat at my friend Louise's kitchen table eating the most amazing gingerbread cookies, I couldn't help but think to myself that I should be putting a few of these bad boys in my pocket to enjoy later on that evening.

Thankfully, as I've gotten older, I've gotten smart enough to know the difference between right and wrong. So instead of loading up, I simply ate all the cookies on the plate.

"Thanks for the cookies!" I said. "They are really good. Sorry for eating them all."

"I'm glad you enjoyed them. My pleasure. I'm pretty much an open book, so ask away."

"Okay. Take me back to growing up. Where did you live? What was it like?"

"I grew up in a small town on the east coast with my brother and my mom, until I was about eight years old," Louise began. "I'm not sure if you knew this, but my biological father passed away from a heart attack. I was only two and half years old, so I don't really remember a lot about him. There are a few things, though, like sitting on his lap reading a book or him speaking to me in French. I was so little. I guess that's why I don't remember much else."

I couldn't help thinking how unfair that must have been for her. Losing a parent isn't the easiest thing to deal with in life, but not knowing them also often creates a void.

However, as Louise shared what she remembered about her father, she didn't seem to have the same deep-seated "fatherly hole" so many people often express. I decided to ask her if she'd ever felt like she had been ripped off from having lost her dad at such a young age.

"No, not at all. I really mean that in a good way. No disrespect to my biological father, but when I was little Mom met and married such an amazing man. I don't feel cheated at all. I actually feel blessed to have him in my life as my dad! I'm so thankful for him."

Intrigued by her comments, I pursued the topic a little further. "What would you say are some of the qualities you really admire about him?"

"He is such a good role model. He is encouraging, kind, and one of the most compassionate people I know. I've never felt like anyone else except his daughter. He has taught me to be strong and to follow through and follow up. He believes in me and is super supportive. There are a lot of things I admire about him. I can tell him anything and I know he'll genuinely listen to me, but probably the one thing that sticks out the most is how he taught me to be compassionate and put family first."

What a great response. Instead of focusing on her loss, she chose to be thankful for the new dad she had been given. Even more impressive was her statement that she had never felt like anyone else but his daughter. Good on him for showing his unconditional love for her, and good on her for accepting it! Love knows no boundaries—but in order for it to be received, it first must be believed!

"What a great acknowledgment of him and your love for him," I said. "Can we explore the idea of him teaching you to put family first?"

"I think you know this, but my mom has struggled with depression, and he has always made sure to get her the help she needs. They say that in the hardest moments the real person comes out, and he has never wavered once. In times when Mom was in her darkest moments, he supported her. He supported us. He made sure that help was available.

He does it in so many different ways, but no matter the circumstance, he has kept our family together because he loves us that much."

The more she shared about him, the more I understood why she had never felt ripped off. His love for all of them truly seemed to have no boundaries.

"Your dad sounds like an amazing man," I said. "Is there anything else in particular you think helps keep you together as a family unit?"

"Yes. If it's been a while since we've all been together, or if we need to have a family meeting, he'd say, 'It's time for a waffle breakfast roll call.' This is a turn-off-your-device time when we all come together for a meal to talk or work things out. It's such great family time and it really does bring us together. I'm thankful for those moments that he helps create. I love them."

Today, social media and other platforms are slowly replacing the traditional ways in which we communicate, and many of us are unknowingly becoming disconnected from each other. We're losing priceless family time.

It's nice to hear that some people are still getting together as a family and having face-to-face dialogue. And based on what Louise has said, she obviously values it.

"What a great idea!" I remarked. "I need to try something like that. It sounds like a great way to proactively create family moments. I have to be honest—if I hadn't had this conversation with you, I would still think you've had the whole world by the tail simply… because your family is very well off."

"No, we're just like everybody else. My mom and dad have also taught me that!"

Funny how sometimes we allow our prejudgments, even the smallest of ones, to form our belief systems. As a society, we have become too willing to believe what social media and other influences tell us. If COVID-19 can teach us anything, it's that in-person family contact is super important. Underneath it all, we're all just like everybody else!

"It's interesting to me that through all your family circumstances, you've taken a thankfulness approach to life," I said. "To what do you attribute that way of thinking?"

"It's going to sound cliché, but I've always looked at my life from the glass-half-full perspective. I see it as a blessing. I know I'm no different than anybody else. Everybody encounters setbacks, and I was taught that life is so much more than that. I journal a lot. I make sure to share and listen with my besties, and I practice self-reflection.

"You know what else has helped change the way I think?" she continued. "A YouTube video called 'It's Not About the Nail.' It's really short, but it definitely helped me become a better listener and communicator. It helped me look at situations differently and ask myself different questions. You should check it out! Good question, by the way. I've never really thought about it before. I guess I just choose to focus on the most important thing to me in my life—my family!"

More often than not, we forget to take the time to self-reflect or pursue tips and strategies for self-improvement. Louise could have chosen to focus on growing up in a single-parent home until her mom met her dad. She could have focused on the depression challenges her family had experienced, but she hadn't. Why? Because cliché or not, she chose to be thankful for all the things in her cup!

"I really do appreciate you sharing a small part of your life with me today," I said. But before we wrap up, I was hoping to ask you a few last questions before I leave with the rest of those cookies!"

"What would you like to know?"

"How has thankfulness helped you throughout your life, and what are you most thankful for?"

She took a moment to gather her thoughts. "Life has been a bit challenging of late, and I don't want my emotions to replace what I really believe. I have to say that throughout my life I've been thankful for the choice to remember all my positive memories. Granted, it isn't always easy, but these memories lighten my heart. I still remember the rough moments, and they allow me to internally work through why they happened and what I can learn from them. I'm thankful for people in my life who recognize who I am as a person and allow me to be who I need to be—me. What many don't know is that at times I'm very much an introvert. I need quiet and personal time to reflect and sometimes decompress. Taking time away helps me to disconnect and recharge. It helps me to get to a good place personally, and by reaching that place I can be the best that others deserve of me. That's important to me, and I'm thankful I have learned to process life this way.

"I was also taught growing up that my feelings matter, and I in turn have always wanted to assist others in knowing that their feelings matter. Acknowledging your feelings has an immense role in acceptance, love for self and for others, as well as individuality. I'm thankful I received that from my family. I'm grateful for the family I've grown with, the family I've been very grateful to create, and the friends in my life that I get to call family. Family is my cornerstone. Even in my moments of loss, in one way or another, they make me feel loved. I am so thankful for family."

Family and the support of family is such an important part of the human experience. We sometimes take our loved ones for granted and give others more of our time than we should. In our fast-paced world, it's so important to connect and take a waffle-breakfast-roll-call approach. It's a great way to start a new tradition.

Chapter Nineteen
Father and Daughter Love

Krista's dad was a man I considered to be among the biggest athletic and coaching influencers in my life. Unfortunately, after graduating from high school, our paths rarely crossed again and I was saddened to learn of his passing. So when the opportunity to reach out to his oldest daughter presented itself, I jumped all over it.

"Thanks for agreeing to meet with me today, Krista. In the end, if it turns out that you're not comfortable with having this published, at least we got to catch up and chat."

"Yes, that's true. I will certainly consider it," she said. "I've always wanted to tell you this. Do you know that when my dad was coaching, he used to talk about how proud he was of you? It sometimes felt like you were a part of our family."

Her comment brought a smile to my face. Her dad had invested countless hours into coaching me without ever expecting anything in return.

"Really? I never knew that," I said. "He was always good to me. Actually, he was the reason I stayed in school. He was the best coach I ever had. He knew I loved sports and he always put in extra time when

I asked. The last time I saw him, I was a student teacher. I wish I could have thanked him properly for his help in those years." I paused. "Are you okay to talk a bit more about your dad and what it was like growing up with him? What was he like as a father?"

"That's complicated. My relationship with my dad went through three different phases—the good, the not-so-good, and then a bit of a hybrid of both. In my younger years, up until age twelve, he was involved and present. When I was little, he always made our bedtime fun and special. He used to tell me and my sister interactive stories where he would trace the path of the characters on our arms until we fell asleep. As I got older, we spent a lot of time as a family outdoors—camping, riding bikes, cross-country skiing, and snowshoeing. One winter, he even built us a full-sized igloo to play in. When we went on road trips, we would sometimes sing in Ukrainian as a family. Those were good years."

Her childhood reflections unexpectedly had generated some strong feelings in her and she had to wipe away a few tears.

"Thank you for asking that question," she said graciously. "I didn't realize it would become so fresh, or so hard to speak about. It's been years, but those are definitely some of my fondest memories of my dad."

"Those moments with your dad seem to bring a real sense of joy to you."

"Yes, for sure. I miss those times, but I guess I just realized that I haven't really thought about them lately. Not sure why, as they're some of my best memories with my dad. They reconnect me to him, in a way. I guess I didn't realize how much I missed him until you asked that question. I don't show a lot of emotion when it comes to him anymore. Our relationship wasn't perfect, by any means. We definitely had our ups and downs, but what relationships don't?"

"No relationship is perfect," I said. "Are you okay to share a little bit about your teenage years? I'm guessing those fall into the not-so-good phase you mentioned earlier."

"My teenage years are where our relationship really changed. He had just been so involved up to that point. Then he became preoccupied with his work, and other things. The only time we spent together was through volleyball and softball. He was a perfectionist, so I felt like I needed to be perfect to earn his love. But I wasn't perfect and felt like there was more criticism than praise. It actually created some anxieties in me! I was hurt, but I just kept it all in. I found ways to manage through those years but we became very distant with each other."

In a time of her life when she should have been receiving his affection and validations, he had sadly became emotionally unavailable. She said it wasn't until her early to mid-twenties that they truly began to reconnect.

"How did you start to re-establish your relationship again?" I asked. "Was there anything in particular that helped you two?"

"He had moved to another province, and it was difficult keeping in touch when we were physically so far apart. And there was a real sense of abandonment on my part. But after a while, our relationship grew and we became closer again. I decided that if I wanted this relationship, I needed to put the past behind me. I decided to focus on our future relationship and my part in it. I can't remember who reached out first, but we started having regular phone calls, stuff like that. He had done a lot of work on himself and was actually interested in what I was doing in my life. There were still ups and downs, but it was nice to have my dad back in my life again."

Relationships can be hard and at times can be complicated. Unfortunately, when those struggles are with the people we love, they are often among the hardest to restore. It was nice to hear that Krista had chosen to forgive and forget in exchange for a second chance at a father-daughter relationship.

"I'm glad you two found a way to work things out. You said that your dad lived out of province, but you began to visit each other and have one-on-one time. What did you mean by that?"

"I would fly there, but when he came here there were no other outside influences. Just us," she said. "That helped us to rediscover our relationship. It was in those times that he told me he was proud of me. Up until then, he had never said that to me. He even wrote me a letter. Our relationship was definitely improving."

Krista's life was hitting its stride on more than one front: her career was flourishing, she was working in a prestigious political position, had recently been selected into a master's program, had graduated from law school, and was now reconciling her relationship with her father.

Unfortunately, it was all interrupted by an unanticipated phone call.

"I will never forget that day," Krista said. "Dad told me he had been diagnosed with stage four colon cancer, and I learned that the survival rate was fifty-fifty. I remember thinking those were good odds, that Dad would make it. It never crossed my mind that he may not."

Sadly, the form of cancer her dad had was more aggressive than expected and his prognosis worsened. Not wanting to lose the time she had left with her father, Krista made the decision to fly out to take care of him as often as possible.

"That must have been really hard on you," I said.

"I don't want this to come out the wrong way, but the few months or so that I got to spend with my dad hold some of my best memories. We talked a lot and had some really great us-time. We ordered pizzas, watched movies, and had father-daughter talks."

"You've mentioned that you also went on long walks, and that you cherish those so much. Can you share a little bit about those moments?"

"For sure. I saw a side of him I'd never paid attention to or recognized before. He always had a smile for people. He could strike up a conversation with anyone and everyone. Not once did he talk about what he was going through. He never let on that he was dying, and at the time that bothered me. I could never understand why he was being so nice and kind to others when he was about to lose his own life. I guess I felt sorry for myself because I was losing my dad. I was watching one of the strongest people I knew deteriorate right in front of my eyes. He refused to complain. Towards the end, I would call him and ask, 'How are you doing today, Dad?' You know what he said? 'Kris, I'm alive. Every day I wake up alive is a good day!' Even when his quality of life seemed so terrible and he couldn't get out of bed, he was still happy to wake up in the morning. Looking back now, I can see how he was still teaching me in his own way."

"Thank you for sharing that with me," I said. "It's very endearing to hear that he never gave up and was still willing to help others. He used to say to me, 'You have so much potential. Never give up. Never!' Those words have carried me for years! Did you ever ask him about his end-of-life approach?"

"Yes, I did one night, when I was rubbing his feet. It helped him to fall asleep."

"What did he say?"

"Dad said, 'Kris, you never know how saying hi to a person or being kind to them may change their day for the better.' That time with him was a real gift to me. I just wish I would have allowed myself to be closer to him long before he became ill. I always thought my family would live to a ripe old age. And then everything changed in one moment. It has caused me to redefine what success means to me. It made me care less about achieving and more about my relationships. It helped me realize that it's my responsibility to make sure I do my part to ensure the relationships in my life remain strong or get better. My relationships are super important to me."

Life is short—and when it's all said and done, all we get to take with us are the memories we've created. What an amazing and beautiful picture of the love between a father and daughter.

"Thank you for sharing your memories of your dad," I said. "I truly do appreciate it. I know you need to get going soon, but I would like to ask you one final question: how has being thankful helped you throughout your life, and what are you most thankful for?"

"I'm most thankful for my family and friends who genuinely care about me and my well-being. Being thankful has caused me to live in the now and appreciate the people in my life. As for how has it helped me? Well, I try at the end of every day to list three to five things I did well, and three to five things for which I am thankful. On bad days, I may be grasping at what might seem like the most minor of things… like, I'm thankful I didn't slip and fall on the terribly icy sidewalk. But taking the time to be thankful makes me realize how lucky I am and that even the worst days have bright spots."

It's never too late to reconnect, build, or rebuild our relationships with the ones we love. Be thankful for them and do your part to ensure your relationships can remain strong or become better.

Chapter Twenty
Vulnerability

Sitting on my couch with a glass of wine in one hand and my phone in the other, I started having an unexpected inner dialogue one evening about vulnerability.

I had often wondered why it's so difficult for most people to let others into their world. Did people feel that their true selves conflicted with society's conforming framework? Was it because they admitting their vulnerability, as children, had been brushed aside by the adults in their lives?

Answers have always escaped me, but one day while mindlessly scrolling my social media accounts, an unexpected opportunity presented itself to me. I noticed a name that I recognized, and she was regularly liking other people's thankfulness and gratitude posts.

At first, I simply dismissed it as coincidence, but I couldn't shake the feeling that I needed to contact her regarding my book project. Even more bizarre was that the conversation I wanted to have with her was about vulnerability.

However, my apparent revelation didn't sit well with the "Poopie Pete" voice in my head. He began asking me questions: *What would you say to someone if they arbitrarily called you and said they felt like they wanted to talk to you about vulnerability? "Sober up, cement head!"*

At first I listened to him, but my gut kept confirming that I needed to make the call. I hadn't listened to my gut in the past, and I always regretted it. So I decided not to miss out on this opportunity. The worst that could happen was that she would unfriend me.

So I chose to be like the topic I wanted to discuss: vulnerable. I crafted my message and then pressed send.

> Me: Hello Stacy, how are you? Haven't seen you in years, but I see you have expanded your family. Congratulations. I know you don't know me very well and this may seem strange, but I am writing a book on thankfulness. I was hoping you would be willing to share your story and perspective for one of the chapters.
>
> Stacy: Hey! Maybe this sounds strange, but I'm currently on a journey of making myself more vulnerable and practicing gratitude daily, so this seems like something that would continue to help me see this through. Can I think about it and get back to you?
>
> Me: Doesn't seem strange at all. Sounds like a chapter. Love it. You have been in my thoughts to ask, but I was hesitant because I barely know you.
>
> Stacy: Glad you asked and made yourself vulnerable. Let's talk in the new year.

After our initial conversation, we tried to connect multiple times, but something always seemed to come up. If we couldn't make it work, it wouldn't be for a lack of trying. I also knew that if we didn't connect, it wasn't supposed to be written.

Thankfully, it was meant to be!

"Hey Stacy, it took a while to connect, but here we are," I said when we began to speak over the phone. "You ready to do this?"

"Yes, I'm glad we are connecting. Sorry for the delay. Life has been pretty crazy lately. How do you want to proceed?

"The interview process is pretty free-flowing. I typically ask questions and just let the conversation go where it needs to go. You good with that?"

"Sounds good. Ask away."

"Perfect, thanks. Let's start with your childhood. How would you describe it in terms of thankfulness?"

"Well, to put it bluntly, I wasn't raised in a thankful environment," Stacy began. "We didn't talk about our feelings ever. It wasn't healthy at all. My parents divorced when I was young and I felt pulled in so many directions. I witnessed affairs and was exposed to verbal manipulation that for years broke my confidence. That was so hard. It took me a long time to come to terms with the trauma I experienced as a child. There was love, but there were also things I never want my children to experience. I realize now that I was in survival mode and scared to be me, because when I was, I wasn't accepted by close members of my family, or it was used against me. It made me wear a mask."

Her response was so real, honest, heartfelt, and vulnerable. I could feel her sadness as she shared her experiences. Her truths were an eye-opener for me, because on the outside she appeared to have everything going for her. She was attractive and smart, had a beautiful family, and financially her life seemed good. But inside, it became very apparent from her sharing that the thing she desired more than anything was to be confident in herself.

"When you say you wore a mask in your childhood, what do you mean by that?"

"I built walls and created systems and structures to appear happy," she said. "The environment in my home stole my confidence. It wasn't a place where I felt I could be vulnerable or express how I truly felt. On the inside I was sad, and so I filled up my life with everything except what I truly wanted. In my adolescent years, I did some things that were a bit unwise. As I look back now, I wonder, what was I thinking? I was lost then and wasn't wise enough to know it."

"So how did you find your way out? Was it a person or a particular event? What helped you?"

"It wasn't one thing, but I would say it was an ongoing combination of people and moments. My dad helping me do my homework really helped me start regaining some of my confidence. I remember it like it was yesterday."

Often in life we forget to ask ourselves proactive, thought-provoking questions like the one I asked Stacy—and we miss out on their power to help us get through challenges. I found it quite interesting that Stacy's response was to bring up a memory that was probably more than twenty years old.

"After he finished helping me, I remember he looked at me with the softest and most caring look and told me how proud of me he was and how smart I was. That's a day I will never forget. I actually got an A on that project. It was the first time I ever remember actually feeling smart. That moment gave me some of my confidence back, because I guess it helped me to believe in myself. When stuff came up or people told me something different, I leaned on that moment."

We often don't recognize the impacts our actions and words have on other people, especially our loved ones. Even though Stacy's dad was probably unaware that she was struggling with her confidence, what he said to his daughter helped her more than he will ever know. It's such a good teaching on choosing our words wisely!

"Very cool. Is there another moment or someone in particular who helped you in becoming you?"

"Yes, my therapist. I got to a spot where I said enough is enough. I couldn't go at this on my own anymore. I decided that if I was going to create and build the life I deserved, I would need a little help to get there. So I began to seek out any resource that would help me regain my confidence, that would allow me to work through becoming more vulnerable. I wanted to be the example for my children that I hadn't had growing up. Counselling has really helped with that."

"How so?"

"Therapy helped me to organize my thought life in a way that made sense to me and share my thoughts with someone I trusted. I tend to stockpile the day-to-day happenings and thoughts in life, so as part of my process I decided to confide in my best friend. I knew she also wanted to talk at a deeper level. So we decided to be there for each other. We also see the same therapist and have been doing so for the past ten years. She is our check in."

The ability to be vulnerable with someone isn't always easy, especially if you didn't learn it as a child or if it was frowned upon. Whether it's a close friend or therapist, the truth is that we all need someone we can trust to share with from time to time.

"I'd like to circle back to our original conversation, if that's okay," I said. "Besides vulnerability, you mentioned that you're currently on a gratitude journey with your friend. Can you tell me more about that?"

"At first, our talks were about the normal things of life. We'd talk about something we were upset about and just needed to get off our chests. Sometimes it was something we struggled to share with our husbands. So we leaned on each other when those moments came up, and honestly it helped us both with our marriages and raising our children. Lately, though, we've noticed our talks involve a lot of complaining, so we said, 'Let's look for things to be thankful for, even if it's something as small as a sip of our morning coffee.'"

I think it's incredible that by becoming vulnerable with the right people, Stacy not only found herself but also brought so many other positives into her life. She admits that she hasn't arrived, but she's thankful that she isn't where she used to be either.

"It's pretty cool that you've found a way to be thankful and vulnerable through a friendship like that," I said. "This has been a really good conversation. Hard to believe that we've been talking for several hours! I do need to ask you a few final questions in order to wrap up our talk, though. Would that be okay?

"Yes, this has been an interesting experience. Thanks for reaching out. I look forward to seeing how you pull all these stories together. What else would you like to know?"

"My final question is, how has being thankful helped you throughout your life and what are you most thankful for?"

"Well, all I know is that gratitude has become my lifeline, especially when life becomes overwhelming. I've made it a point to practice gratitude. I believe that when people endure emotional trauma like I have, they can allow it to swallow them whole, or they can run towards it. I have done both. In my experience, being thankful has made handling my past trauma more manageable and has definitely softened my pain. As odd as this may sound to some people, I'm also thankful for the lessons I've learned from my trauma. My emotional wounds have served me in unexplainable ways; they have made me stronger, more resilient, and confident in my abilities as a person, allowing me to delve deeper into the true meaning of gratitude and how important it really is. For that, I am eternally thankful."

Her journey into vulnerability isn't over, but with the help of thankfulness, therapy, and her best friend, Stacy is now better equipped to be open and vulnerable with the ones she loves.

Chapter Twenty-One
A Friend Like Kelsey

So there I was in the exact same restaurant, sitting at the exact same table, at the exact same time of day, about to do another interview for the Thankfulness Project. Except this time, there was one major difference: I didn't have any misgivings about my journey. Nor was I concerned that the person I was about to interview had been referred to me by Stacy. In fact, it was Stacy's best friend!

"Hi Derek, I'm Kelsey," the woman said when she sat down. Nice to meet you. How are you?"

"I'm well. Thanks for asking. It's kind of unusual how things come together, isn't it?"

"I've heard it said, 'Put it out there in the universe and it will come back to you.' I believe that is what is happening with me participating in your project. Stacy and I have been practicing being thankful for years on our own and together. It has helped us both so much. I'm curious about all the stories and seeing how you pull this together."

It was funny how she said exactly the same thing Stacy had. To be completely honest, at that point in my journey I, too, was interested in how the final project would come together. All I knew for sure was that if I trusted what my gut was telling me and pursued the thankfulness opportunities I was being gifted with, the rest would work itself out.

"You ready, Kelsey?"

"I'm a bit nervous, but yes, let's start."

"Don't be. It's really just a conversation. How about we start with how you met your best friend."

"Sounds good. Let me think. Stacy and I lived in the same apartment block and always seemed to run into each other there. We hung out in the same social circles, but for the most part our early friendship was superficial. We always seemed to be in a group of three to five women who got along well. But if I'm being honest, larger groups of women can become tiring because we're so busy trying to build consensus so we don't offend one another. You use hedge words like 'maybe' or 'could' instead of sharing your honest opinion. But with Stacy, there was something different—in a good way. She was more open and real. I liked that about her."

As I listened to her explain the dynamics involved in the early stages of her friendship with Stacy, it was a good reminder that relationships take time and effort.

I once heard a speaker say there are four kinds of friends. The acquaintance—you say hi or bye to them daily, but that's the extent of it. The half-friend—you may go for lunch or hang out in the same circles, but they're not the sort of person you'd invite over to your home for one-on-one conversations. A true friend—a person you can confide in from time to time, and when you do, you know that they'll support you. Finally, there's an intimate friend—a person you can share everything with, who sticks by you through thick and thin, forgives, and is genuinely excited for you when life goes well but also confronts you when your choices don't reflect the real you.

Over the years, Kelsey and Stacy had obviously built an amazing friendship to the point that their friendship embodied all four stages. But I was keenly interested to learn more about how they'd gotten to the intimate friend stage.

"What do you think helped the two of you build your friendship to the point that you became the best friends you are today?"

"That's a really good question. One thing we did for sure was making sure we made time for each other regularly. At first it wasn't easy, but if we didn't connect we both understood that it wasn't personal. We promised each other that no matter what was going on in our lives, we would always make time for one another—and we did, even after we got married. Whether it was a quick call or a morning message, we kept our promises. We shared things and were honest with each other. That definitely helped us to establish a good level of trust. I felt like she had my back and vice versa. Looking back now, that's how we built such a wonderful friendship."

For some reason, I couldn't seem to shake the feeling that I should follow up even further. So instead of asking questions that may have taken us in a different direction, I dug a little deeper.

"She's your best friend today, but good friendships don't often come without a few challenges," I said. "What were they for you two?"

"We've had a couple of small ones. And one that neither of us could have anticipated. Several years ago, we both discovered we were pregnant and had similar due dates. We were so excited to be going through that experience together and planned out the experience from beginning to end. We talked every day and were going to share all our belly pictures with each other and our ideas for the babies' rooms. It seemed like we were always talking on the phone. It was a happy time, for sure… and then I had a miscarriage."

There are times in life when you don't know what to say or do, and this moment was one of them for me. I wanted to respond in a genuine way, but I also wanted to let her share. So I decided to zip my lips and let her say whatever she was willing to in that moment.

"I was heartbroken," she continued after a short pause. "I was so upset. It wasn't fair. I wanted to be happy for her. I mean, I was, but at the time I guess grief was getting the best of me. Seeing the pictures of her growing tummy, and knowing I should also be sharing in those moments, was really hard for a while. My mental health wasn't in a good spot. I wanted to be a good friend, but I was struggling emotionally and not sure how to share that."

Losing a pregnancy and dealing with the emotional challenges that brings on is something no family should have to go through.

Broken, lost, confused, and struggling emotionally, she did the only thing that she could think of: she reached out for help. Counselling had assisted her before, and she hoped it would do the same thing again.

"It was a trying time, and it wasn't easy, but I have been able to work through it. My counselor listened in a way others couldn't, or didn't know how to. At the time I felt so alone. I was hurting so much. I really needed to release all the thoughts and struggles that were going on inside me. She helped me come through it and I was eventually able to deal with what happened and regain my thought life again."

"That must have been an unbelievable challenge to overcome."

"It was. It wasn't something I expected I would ever go through. Nor would I wish it on anybody. I'm okay now. It definitely was hard on all my relationships."

The pain that's often associated with traumatic experiences isn't something that necessarily goes away or is fully healed because of counselling. But talking and getting advice from a friend or professional can assist a person in making it a little more tolerable. Everyone heals differently. Recovering from loss isn't a sprint. That said, the process can be expedited to overcome the snake that bit you through the antidote of thankfulness.

"I'm amazed at your resiliency to find the strength to reach out as part of your healing process," I said. "I know you said it was hard on your relationships, and I understand why. Can I ask about what helped you to reconnect with Stacy?"

"We connected not long after. I remember sitting at home reflecting on everything that had transpired with me, between us and with myself. That's when I had my Aha! moment. She was my best friend and I missed her. I thought that if I didn't know what to say or do, she probably didn't know what to say either. I looked at it from her perspective for the first time and knew I needed to reach out to her. I'm so thankful I did."

Through both of their efforts, they mended the misunderstandings. Today Kelsey says they are as close as they have ever been.

"Thank you for trusting me with your very personal story," I said. "It's been a pleasure interviewing you. I do have two final questions, though. If you could tell your best friend what your friendship means to you, what would you say? And my other question is, how has being thankful helped you throughout life and what are you most thankful for?"

"Those are great questions! Give me a moment. Actually, I really want to think about how I respond. Can I email my responses to you?"

"Yes, that works. Send them whenever you are ready."

As promised, I received the below responses to my final questions a few days later.

> Stacy feels like home. She is my non-judgmental confidant, giving me my best advice on all things from boys to babies to blazers, my ally, my sweeter self, my mentor, my mood booster, my reflection when I'm lacking self-awareness and my elbow nudge when I need it.
>
> As for what I'm thankful for? Definitely my education—and not just in the most traditional sense of the word, but bigger picture, enlightenment. I'm thankful for schoolteachers of early grades and later years alike who encouraged me to succeed through their mentorship and attentiveness. I'm thankful for jobs that socialized and humbled me, for friendships that embraced me with empathy, for relationships that pushed me into uncomfortable places and made me witness my own inner strength. I'm thankful for yoga, which taught me to be patient with myself, lean in to the moment, and breathe through the discomfort. Traveling opened my eyes to a world beyond, and therapy opened my ears to the voice inside. I'm thankful for reading, which empowered me with the pleasure of escape and intelligent conversation. And I'm also thankful for a husband who loves me despite all my dark corners. Lastly, motherhood has gifted me the purest form of love and challenges me every day to be my best self yet.

Building and maintaining a true friendship requires everyone involved to put the work into achieving it. Be a friend like Kelsey and make the effort. You won't be disappointed that you did.

Chapter Twenty-Two
The "F" Word

Alice is a person I have always admired. We've been friends for years, and even though we rarely see each other, when we do reconnect I always leave our conversations feeling thankful that she is in my life. So I reached out and asked her to participate in the project. She graciously said yes.

"Thank you for agreeing to be part of this journey, Alice," I said to the woman sitting across from me. "It really is just a conversation about life. If something grabs my attention or really resonates with me, I may dig deeper into that area if that's okay with you. Sound good?"

"Yes, sounds good. I really don't think I have much of a story, but ask away."

"How about we start with your life growing up? What was your childhood like?"

"Well, I was the oldest in a time when there was always something to be done and I was expected to do it. I really didn't have much of a traditional childhood. It was hard!"

What did she mean by not having a traditional childhood? I assumed she had to help out a lot on the farm where she grew up, like many farm kids do, but it was obvious by her tone of voice that she had experienced a real sense of loss.

"Alice, you said you didn't have a traditional childhood. Can you tell me a bit more about that? What did a typical day look like for you back then?"

"Sure. There was love, but I was always working. From as early as I can remember, I cooked, cleaned, and looked after my siblings. There was no time for play. Something always needed to be done in order for our family to make it day in and day out. Sometimes it was going out to gather eggs, but other times it was actually getting the chicken for dinner and fully preparing it, start to finish, the whole nine yards. You name it, I did it. My parents both worked, so I was the only option. If I didn't do it or coordinate it, it wouldn't get done. We needed to eat and to live! I know it was different times back then, but to be honest it wasn't really a choice. I was the oldest and it was my responsibility to help provide for the family."

As she told me her story, I came to better understand her disappointment over not really being able to be "just a kid." I also better understood why whenever I was around her, she never sat down. It was as if she felt the need to always be doing something. Whether it was with her family, at her job, or her endless volunteering to help others, she never sat still.

"That must have been trying for you, especially because you were a child yourself," I said. "Playing is a big part of growing up. Did you resent what was being asked of you at such a young age?"

"At the time, yes, for sure… but not now. When I was younger, I never looked at what my parents were teaching me; I looked at what I thought they weren't giving me. The one thing I never learned to do was relax. In my mind, there is always something to do. After all these years, I've finally said enough is enough. I'm taking the time. Even if it's just to sit down for thirty minutes and watch a show, I'm doing it. I realize I do need the me-time thing."

Most women today work, manage a home and children, and far too often forget how crucial it is to stop *doing* and just *be*. I was encouraged that Alice was choosing to view her experience as a teaching moment instead of as a woe-is-me, unfair thought process.

"Your perspective is inspiring, and it's good to hear that you've created the me-time habit for yourself. You definitely deserve it."

"Thank you. It's difficult sometimes but I'm a work in progress."

"Can we talk a little more about your untraditional childhood? Other than 'adulting' at such a young age, was life good otherwise?"

"Yes, it was good. There were some other obstacles, but I don't wish to discuss them. The past is the past. They are now between me and the Lord! I actually haven't thought about my frustrations from back then in a very long time. As a child, I did witness stuff I shouldn't have. It made me so angry for years, but over time I've dealt with it. Don't get me wrong—I'm thankful for what both my parents taught me, but back then there was so much going on and I found it hard to handle."

I could tell that Alice had tapped into a part of her memory that had been dormant for quite some time. So instead of probing those challenging times further, I steered our conversation back to what she'd done to overcome them.

"You said earlier that you couldn't wait to get out of there. You obviously did. Where did you go?"

"I wanted a life of my own, so I went off to school to get a career. I was angry on the inside but didn't realize how mad I was until I accomplished my goals. Achieving them was good for me, but it didn't stop that knot in my stomach. It was like it was always there waiting to remind me of my lost childhood."

At one time or another, we all experience circumstances that cause us to become internally discontent, bitter even. As Alice pointed out, achieving your goals may be important, but chasing them isn't the solution to addressing or bringing closure to your past hurts.

"You moved on and established a new life for yourself like you wanted to," I said. "Did doing that help you to overcome your past anger towards parts of your childhood?

"No, they didn't. They just silenced it for a while. I was proud of what I had accomplished, but it didn't change the way I felt about what I had witnessed. Looking back now, I realize that I was just playing the shell game. In a lot of ways, I was avoiding my childhood disappointments by doing things or avoiding anything or anyone that associated me with those times."

She had accomplished so much—purchased her first home, got married, ran a business, and started a family of her own, but her past still found ways to control her emotions.

"Alice, I see you as a role model and a very successful woman in all areas of your life, not just financial. You obviously have come to terms with your past resentments, and I'm interested in knowing what helped you."

She smiled. "I knew those experiences had made me bitter. All I can tell you is that after I was introduced to God and the world of forgiveness, I embraced it and was finally able to see things differently. What can I say? The rest is history. When I learned more about what forgiveness means, it opened me up to thinking differently. For the first time I understood that forgiveness was for me and not the situations or people that had hurt me. It definitely was a process, but I'm so glad I chose to forgive myself and others. It took a huge weight off my shoulders. At some point, it hit me that it was simply poor decisions on the part of people that had hurt me. We all make bad choices, including me. Between my husband, my faith, and myself, I was able to work through it and forgive. It set me free. That's the power in forgiveness. It lets you move on."

Often we think that if we forgive someone, it somehow absolves the other person of their actions. This isn't true. Nor do we have to allow those people back into our lives. Forgiveness simply is that gift to ourselves which cuts the umbilical cord to the unhealthy anger, bitterness, and resentment that has unfairly been brought into our lives. As Alice said, "It lets you move on."

"I couldn't help but notice the huge smile you had on your face when you had your forgiveness Aha! moment. I'm guessing that is the reasoning for your change of perspective on your childhood now."

"Absolutely! Looking back, I know that if I looked harder I would have realized that I was also receiving so many good things in those days, especially from my mom! She taught me how to be a strong woman. She was the leader in our home. She was a visionary! I see that now. No doubt about that. She made things happen. I learned to stick up for myself because of her and to work hard. She taught me that you can always help someone, that it isn't about how much money you have, and that the most important things people need usually aren't financial. No matter what your circumstance, there is always someone else who's worse off, so count your blessings and be a helper."

What a powerful revelation. What wisdom! Instead of looking at her personal circumstances through a negative lens, she chose to take those lessons and grow from the experience.

"There sure is a lot of wisdom in what you just said," I remarked. "Are there any other thoughts you'd like to share that helped you become the woman you are today?

"Forgiveness, faith, friends, and family all played a role in who I am today. I'm thankful I can still have joy. I discovered years ago that life isn't about what happens to you. It's what you do with what happens to you. Be thankful in all things. God wants the best for all of us. We need to quit living in past hurts or struggles and live the abundant life we have been given."

I never thought I would say this but it sure seemed like the F-word—forgiveness—had the power to give us back our lives.

"Outside of forgiveness, has thankfulness played a part in your life?"

"Absolutely," she said. "No matter what happens in life, there's always something you can choose to be thankful for. We just need to realize what's important to us and let that become part of the influence in the lives we create."

"I agree. Very well said. I have one last question I'd like to ask you before I wrap up our interview. What would you say you're most thankful for, and how has it helped you throughout your life?"

"When I look at what others have gone through, it makes me see how truly blessed my life has been. That's how it has helped me. You know, Derek, you don't have to look very far to see others in more pain and tougher circumstances than either of us have experienced! That's why appreciating people and showing them the love you have for them is so important. As for what I'm most thankful for, that's a tough question because I am so thankful for so many things. But finding a way in which I can forgive and let go is definitely one of the things I'm most thankful for! Finding out it was possible to let those who hurt me off the hook has been a Godsend. Forgiveness and the Lord have helped me to disconnect and sever those pains and any bitterness I have experienced in my life. I'm very thankful for forgiveness and that it found me!"

Practicing forgiveness and choosing to be thankful helped Alice move forward to let go of the past hurts that were controlling her. It wasn't a quick fix, but it definitely was worth her effort.

Chapter Twenty-Three
A Selfless Life

I was introduced to Katie through a mutual friend who told me that Katie would be an awesome person to contact regarding this book project. I hadn't met her before, but after some reflection I decided to make contact. As she lived out of province, we agreed to do the interview by telephone.

"Hi Katie," I greeted the woman on the other end of the line. "Thanks for agreeing to participate."

"You're welcome. It sounds like an interesting journey you're on. I am glad to offer whatever I can."

"I sure am learning a lot! You ready to get started? Can you tell me a little bit about your childhood?"

"I was born in Ottawa, and then we moved to Toronto when I was six years old. Most of my childhood was spent there."

"Why Toronto?"

"We moved there after my father retired from the military," Katie said. "I loved living in Toronto, but in my teenage years I did struggle finding my way."

"Was it because of the typical teenage struggles or was there something else?"

"Some of it was adolescence, but I also lost my father when I was thirteen. He died from a blood clot in his brain. He was only fifty-three years old. After that, the last of my siblings moved out and that made me feel even more alone. My mom really had a tough time coping with the loss of my father. She was traumatized and I believe she became depressed. I felt like I had nowhere to turn to for support or guidance. I had older siblings, but they had either moved out or gotten married. So that just left me with my mom and I felt so alone."

Katie had been saddled with some of life's hardest moments at such a young age. Grieving the loss of a parent is hard enough, but grieving it on your own is even harder. Especially when you're only thirteen!

"That must have been really hard. How did you manage through those times?"

"At the time I didn't realize I was lost, but looking back I realize now that I was. I just remember feeling like there was nobody pulling for me. I just wanted support and direction, but because Mom was struggling herself, I never received either. I'm not sure how I got through my grief. I guess I just went through the motions. I was too young to understand that I didn't know what I didn't know. I do know that I felt like I didn't really have a purpose."

Without the proper guidance and support systems in place, many young people struggle to deal with their grief, or struggle to understand why they feel a certain way. It's hard to find a sense of purpose when you can't see the forest for the trees.

"What did you do after high school was done?" I asked.

"To be honest, I was tired of the single life, of being lonely. I wanted to settle down and have a family of my own. I met a man and we got married when I was twenty-one. I moved out of the city and was pregnant a couple of months later while helping to raise his three children. It was all a bit overwhelming. I wasn't prepared for so many changes at one time. I kind of felt like all the walls of the world had closed in on me. I never really told anybody, because at the time I didn't understand what I was going through myself."

Young, with a new husband, new family, new baby and feeling like she was a bit of an island to herself, she needed something or someone to intervene. Little did she know that peace and purpose was just around the corner.

"Those overwhelming changes stole something from me," Katie continued. "Nothing I did seemed to be able to change that feeling, until I heard the gospel for the first time. All I know is that I discovered there was a better life available for me with God. It breathed life into my soul. It was a pivotal, life-changing moment that gave me a solid foundation on which to start building. It caused me to want to start to make some life changes. It truly gave me peace, hope, joy, and purpose. I finally discovered that God really loved me right where I was and had a plan for my life. As soon as I understood that, I never looked back."

Love was her passion for her truth. Faith found her, or maybe she found faith. Either way, it was exactly what she needed—an antidote to overcome her overwhelming feelings and eventually get her life back.

"I like how fired up you were when you told me about finding God and how it changed your perspective," I said. "Such a great attitude."

"Funny you say that. I love my faith, but you know what? It's also about your attitude. I have this great quote from Chuck Swindoll that I found. I try to live by it every day. He says that life is ten percent what happens to you and ninety percent how you choose to handle it. You know, it's so true. I lost my son Cole three years ago and the fact that I understood what he meant gave me the strength and courage I needed to breathe every day."

"How did he pass away?"

"Doing what he loved. He and a couple of humanitarians flew out from Puerto Plata to Port-au-Prince. They were taking medical supplies to Hurricane Mathew victims. They ended up returning later than planned and flew into one of the worst electrical storms that area has experienced in twelve years. The plane went down, killing everyone onboard, including Cole."

I believe that when you lose a child, or anything important to you in life, there's no way to get through it quickly. It's a daily ongoing process.

You need to find a way to embrace the memories you hold so dearly. Katie is a great example of that.

"I'm sorry for your loss, Katie. Are you okay to continue?"

"Yes. It isn't always easy to talk about losing him, but you know what really helps me to handle it? My faith! I'm so thankful for my faith and fully knowing that I will see him again one day. You also need to stay thankful and positive. Early on after we lost Cole, I decided that I could either put my thumb in my mouth, get in the fetal position and cry for the rest of my life, or be thankful for the time we had together with him and honor my son. We were blessed to have him for thirty-six years. He really was an outstanding and selfless human being. He was fully committed to giving his time and efforts to humanitarian work."

What brave, wise, and insightful statements. It was encouraging to hear how she had chosen to trust what she believed so she could keep moving forward and honor her son's legacy of love.

"I heard from a friend that Cole also started a social enterprise company called Cambio Goods," I said. "Could you tell me a little about that?"

"Certainly. Cole was always trying to figure out ways to help less fortunate people. He used to tell me, 'I don't believe our generation has the luxury not to care.' He fully understood that being born in North America was by chance, and he was going to take every opportunity to use that gift he had received to help others. He began working with Live Different, building homes for the impoverished in the Dominican Republic, and experienced firsthand their extreme poverty. After that, he ventured into Haiti and helped build a school that now has almost four hundred students. That school meant the world to him. It was one of the highlights of his life. He really did believe in education and that it's one of the keys to get out of poverty. When he went back to the Dominican, he met a craftsman and really wanted to help him help himself. They began to collaborate and they came up with an idea to make designer purses and bags that would appeal to a broader audience. It worked. This has allowed for the craftsman and other young men to be employed. That's how Cambio was started."

"Wow. Your son sounds like an amazingly kind and loving person. What does Cambio mean?"

"It means change. Exactly what Cole was striving to bring into people's lives. Music producer David Foster even participated on one of the builds he led. That was a real highlight for Cole. Mr. Foster invited Cole to come to his gala to photograph Seal and Michael Bolton."

Cole had injected love into everything he touched. As a matter of fact, Katie told me that someone once said to her, "Everything he touched he made beautiful." To say this guy was selfless is an understatement. And after talking with Katie, it became obvious to me that the apple hadn't fallen far from the tree.

"I was told that after Cole's passing, you and your husband continued on with Cole's humanitarian work through Cambio Goods. Can you tell me about how that came to be?"

"That hadn't been our plan at all, but we decided that we wanted to honor his life and continue what he'd started, because it was supporting people. His dreams were too beautiful to stop. It was a way for us to help continue with all of what he had given his life to. People's lives are still being made better because of his heart for people. Can I share one more thing that helps me to continue what I do?"

"Please do."

"I was at a furniture store looking to buy an armchair. I walked past a woman and she said to me, 'You are a women of great taste' and then pointed at my handbag. It was one of the Cambio purses. To know he's still touching people, and that the love he left behind is still being felt, warmed my heart. I actually told her the whole story and we cried together. I've experienced that same scenario hundreds of times in my life."

"Thank you again for sharing with me today," I said. "Before I let you go I have one last question for you. How would you say being thankful has helped you in your journey throughout your life, and what are you most thankful for?"

"Great question. Truthfully, I'm thankful for every day and will never take life for granted. That gift of thankfulness comes as a direct result of my faith in God. I've discovered that being thankful is the essence of your life. Cole was a gift, and so was his life. All life is a gift.

The moments we had with him in our family, I will forever cherish. We are so very thankful for Cole, his life, and his legacy. I am also very thankful for all of my children and the time I've been given with them. I can't imagine not being thankful for it. As for being thankful, it puts everything else into perspective. It makes you realize how precious life is. Life is so brief. You really need to make the most of it in all that you do, because everything can change in an instant."

Cole and Katie's selfless way of living is such a good example of what love can do. Katie discovered that being thankful is the essence of your life. I hope this story inspires you to discover the same.

Chapter Twenty-Four
Believing in Yourself

With the deadline of my year-long thankfulness project quickly closing in, I started to wonder who the last story would be about. Would it be one of the original people who had committed to being part of the project or would it be someone I had wanted to write about but never reached out to? Either way, all I knew for sure was that it would be exactly who it needed to be.

"How are you making out with your interviews?" asked Sheila North, the person who I'd interviewed first on this long journey.

"Pretty good, thanks for asking. Hard to believe it started with you and now I'm down to my final few. I'm still hoping to speak with Janis Kelly, the Olympian."

"Have you reached out to her? She is super nice. I'm sure she would participate."

"No, I haven't," I said. "I'm still kicking myself for not approaching her when she spoke to that group of students at the Live Different event at South East Collegiate. Her message really stayed with me. You don't happen to have her contact info, do you?"

"Sorry, I don't. The last I heard was that she had taken a job on the east coast. I don't even have her phone number anymore."

I smiled, but on the inside a sense of disappointment washed over me. I had hoped to interview Janis, but for some reason I'd neglected to reach out when the opportunity presented itself.

Rather than dwelling on my lost opportunity, I decided to follow up with the people who had originally responded to me. With a new plan mapped out, I shut down my writing for the rest of the day and proceeded to do the next craziest thing next to deciding to write a book—I headed to Costco to shop on a weekend!

As I pulled into the parking lot, I was pleasantly surprised. There was no "Poopie Pete" honking his horn continuously because the person backing out of their parking stall was taking way too long. Nor was there any sign of Mr. Best Parking Lot Driver Ever flipping people the bird. A small miracle to say the least!

Entering the building, I flashed my Costco card to the attendant at the door and then quickly made my way through the semi-crowded aisles to grab my usual items.

As I walked past the meat section, a woman to my left suddenly caught my attention. I couldn't believe my eyes. Perplexed, I moved in for a closer look, and to my surprise and delight it was Janis Kelly! Not willing to miss my opportunity to speak with her again about the project, I quickly regained my composure and walked over to her.

"Hi, you may have noticed me following you for a bit, but it's for a good reason," I opened. "Are you Janis Kelly?"

Laughing, she said, "Yes, that's me. My niece did say she thought you were following us. How are you? What can I do for you?"

"Sorry about that. I've been wanting to speak with you about participating in a book I'm writing by contributing an interview. I had asked Sheila North for your contact information, but she said that she'd lost touch with you and believed you were living out east. I just texted her a few minutes ago and said, 'You're not going to believe who I ran into at Costco.' She encouraged me to approach you. My name is Derek."

"Wow, very cool," Janis said. "I actually just moved back to Winnipeg and I'm getting settled in. Your project sounds intriguing. You know what? Send me a sample and the purpose for the book and I'll get back to you."

We exchanged numbers, but as I was driving home it dawned on me that again my hope was about to turn into reality. I concluded that only the big guy in the sky could have orchestrated such a meeting. So instead of worrying whether she would agree, I simply thanked God for making the encounter happen.

Several weeks passed and I still hadn't heard back from her. There was snow on the ground and Rudolph was only weeks away from flying the bearded wonder around the globe. I was sure our paths crossing hadn't been a coincidence, but I also knew that sometimes people get busy with life and forget to respond. Everything inside me told me my encounter with Janis hadn't been an accident, so I decided to follow up one last time.

Well, you guessed it—she replied back with a time and date. Needless to say, I was happier than Donald Trump when his combover stays in place.

"Hi Janis," I said when we finally met. "Thank you for doing this. I still can't believe it worked out the way it did."

"Yes, this is perfect timing for me." Her smile could have filled the room. "Life has been quite hectic lately. I had just told my friend that something like this was exactly what I needed. How do you want to start?"

"We're just going to have a conversation, and I will guide it. My hope is that someone else will read your story and it will encourage or empower them in their journey through life. Sound good?"

At first we talked about everything and anything, but eventually we got to a place where she was comfortable enough to share some of her personal life.

"You mentioned you have a twin brother," I said. "Can you tell me a little about him?"

"I just love him, I really do. He is such an amazing and awesome person."

"It's nice to see how much you appreciate the blessings that can come from having such a large family. You've probably been asked this a million times, but I would really like to know: when did you realize you were a gifted volleyball player?"

"I didn't really start to play volleyball until high school. In junior high, we didn't have enough players to form a team. But I do remember enjoying volleyball in gym class."

"Can you tell me about that time?"

"It was when I started playing any type of organized sports. I had such amazing teachers back then who allowed us to just play and have fun. My gym teacher, Miss Joyal, told me that if I worked hard, I would be really good one day. She could see that I could jump and that I really enjoyed playing. That's what started it for me. It helped me feel good about myself and come out of my shell. I used to walk around with my head down and cover my smile, but volleyball gave me a sense of worth. It was also a great energy release for me."

Anyone who's ever seen Janis play can tell you that her potential was undeniably elite. That said, potential is nothing unless it's nurtured and acted upon. It was nice to hear her give kudos to those who had originally encouraged her to develop her love for the game.

"I really enjoyed playing sports," she continued. "I liked the competition and interaction with my teammates. It was a great experience and a lot of fun. At the time, I didn't realize how many people were helping me along the way. Great teachers, coaches, and people like Amy and Anna's mom were all there behind the scenes without expecting anything in return. They made it possible to play the game I grew to love."

Amy and Anna's mom? Who were they? I asked her about who these people were, and what role they'd played in her love for the game. It turned out that Amy and Anna had been her teammates.

"The first year I played club volleyball, I hadn't realized there were weekend tournaments. The games lasted all day, so Amy and Anna's mom always brought extra sandwiches and food to our games. Looking back, I realize they had probably packed extras for me. Reflecting on those times, I recognized other moments when people were looking out for me. I always assumed there were no fees to play club volleyball, but as I got older I understood that someone had paid those fees for me.

Without their generosity, I couldn't have afforded to play. There are a lot of good people out there. People are good and kind. If you don't look around, you'll miss the good things they do. I'm thankful for all of them."

I was moved by the good people in her life who had chosen to be so generous. A lot of people say things like "If you can be anything, be kind," but it was great to hear a story about those words being put into action.

"What happened after high school volleyball?" I asked.

"I wasn't recruited out of high school. I ended up walking on to try out at the University of Winnipeg. I made the team and they offered me a scholarship."

I couldn't believe that one of the best high school players in Manitoba, and probably Canada, hadn't been recruited. Regardless, it goes to show that if you follow up on your passion, you can end up with a positive result.

Unfortunately, her university experience almost made her quit the game she loved so much.

"I was young, raw, strong-willed, and knew I had to prove that I deserved to be there," she said. "I put in a lot of time. I worked really hard, but the coach at the time didn't fully believe in me. It was hard. I cried a lot. I continued to work hard, but it never seemed to be enough for the coach and caused me to doubt myself. Deep down, I knew he was wrong, but it made me strongly consider walking away from the game forever."

I hadn't expected to hear this from the Canadian Volleyball Hall of Famer. Ironically, just when it seemed like she would never play again, the head coach of the Canadian women's National team reached out.

"Mike Burchuk invited me to try out, but I told him I was no longer playing. He suggested that I come to the tryout anyway. So I went. One of the first drills of that tryout was me hitting against the towering block of Christine Toews and Lisa Kachkowski. My first hit, they stuffed me. I was determined to prove myself, so I stayed and later made the team."

Her humility was inspiring. She not only made the team, she went on to play for Team Canada in the 1996 Summer Olympics in Atlanta and was a successful pro on several international teams for more than ten years. She is without a doubt one of the top female volleyball players Canada has ever produced. More recently, she was inducted into the Canadian Volleyball Association Hall of Fame.

"Besides your sheer determination and talent, what do you remember about your coach, Mike Burchuk?"

"As a coach, Mike pushed hard, but I always knew he believed in me. He was the strict and structured coach I needed at that time. He challenged and continually motivated me. He brought out the best in me. He taught me hitting consistency, and helped me increase my vertical and the attitude to go out hard. He taught us to be psychologically tough and gave us a toolbox of skills to draw from. The thing I valued most was that he expected our best. If we were sick and could only give seventy percent, he embraced that and expected it. He taught me to take pride in little successes, but not to be satisfied by them. I learned that if you do all you can and believe in yourself, amazing things can happen. He is up there as one of my biggest influences in life."

The words that other people speak into our lives have a power very few fully appreciate. When we allow these words into our hearts, they create beliefs that end up influencing so much of the way we think. That's why, like Janis, it's so important to reflect on them and follow our hearts.

"Thank you for giving me a glimpse into your life and storied career," I said. "Believing in yourself is so important, but it was nice to hear you being so thankful for the many influencers in your life. Looking back over your life, you have accomplished some pretty amazing things. How has being thankful helped you and what are you most thankful for?"

"You know, the person who truly gave me strength is my mom," Janis told me. "She is my role model. I'm so thankful for what I've learned from her by watching, feeling, and living. I remember Mom getting up every day and working from 6:00 a.m. to 6:00 p.m. to take care of us. She was in the kitchen cooking before we even got out of bed. She worked so hard and led by example. My mom is amazing. She inspires me. My dad was a role model, too, but in a different way. He taught us to always do our best.

"I'm thankful for each lesson and each moment, good or bad, that sport has given me. The lessons all taught me something about life. Sport taught me to reach past myself. It gave me confidence and helped me become who I am today. It taught me to get along and work with others, to be a team player, and to find a way. When I'm down, when I'm faced with adversity, stress, or a challenge, I can have what I call a 'funk day.' But after that, I move on. Great people, great friendships, and being thankful has made me who I am today."

Your belief system is a powerful influencer in what you will or will not achieve in life. What you believe, you often receive. That being said, be thankful for those who truly help you to grow, believe in yourself, and be willing to put in the hard work that is required to achieve your goals—because if you do, anything is possible.

Chapter Twenty-Five
The Best Mom Ever

As the last chapter, I would like to honor the most selfless, kind, giving, and thankful woman I know: my mother. She has no idea I've included her as the last story, nor did I interview her for it. The truth is that I didn't need to.

Instead I've chosen to use a reflection I first wrote on March 7, 2019. Her part in the story isn't very big, but I truly believe it exemplifies what living a thankful life really means.

Weeks prior to departing for a series of business meetings outside the city, I felt the need to tell one of my staff to rent her own vehicle instead of travelling with me. I had another meeting the following day and had decided I would handle it on my own. In all the years I've been in management, I'd never done that.

On the day of our departure, the roads were clear. I was happy to be making the trip, and I'd even been upgraded to a better vehicle which had a higher safety rating. I didn't fully appreciate the gesture.

In hindsight, I had no idea how important that simple act of kindness from the manager of the rental car company would be for me.

Several hours into the trip, the male in me started to explore the multitude of mystery buttons on my steering wheel. I wasn't fully able to understand or use all the options I found, but one called "lane assist" had begun to really solicit my attention.

After messing around with it for a couple of minutes, I discovered that one of its main functions was to keep the car between the highway lines while driving. It even worked if you took your hands off the wheel. So like the kid I am, I began testing it out. To my surprise, it did exactly what it said it would do, even while rounding a curve in the road. I was so impressed that I decided to engage the technology for the duration of my trip.

As I passed the halfway point of my journey, I began to daydream about the spicy chicken wings I would be eating in a few more hours. I was in my happy place and immediately began trying to add even more happiness by searching for a good old rock n' roll song on the radio. As I scrolled through the various stations, I came across one of them playing ACDC's "Thunderstruck." So I did what all mid-forties rockers would do: I cranked it up.

Minutes later, my bliss was interrupted by an oncoming car which had suddenly entered my lane. With no time to react, I grabbed the wheel to brace for impact and then *wham!* I found myself in a real-life "Thuderstruck" moment.

As my car spun out of control from the impact of two vehicles colliding head-on at more than a hundred kilometers per hour, my thoughts went into slow motion. One voice began saying, "This is it." While the other told me, "Hold on."

As fast as it had all begun, it stopped and my experience went from warp speed to complete tranquility. Surrounded by clouds, I heard no sounds and felt no pain, it was as if I had been transported to lala land.

I'm not sure how long I stayed there, but eventually my Matrix-like experience came to an end and I found myself randomly speaking out loud. To this day, I'm not sure who I was talking to, but I do know the first words out of my mouth were "Am I dead?" Those words must have held some type of power, because it seemed that as soon as I said them, all my senses downloaded back into me. Suddenly, I fully knew where

I was—in the driver's seat—and yes, I was still alive. So I lifted up the airbag covering my door and exited what was left of the vehicle.

Ambulances were on the scene in an instant. I was rushed to a nearby hospital and treated for a few cuts, bruises, whiplash, and a broken knuckle and then told I was free to go.

My mom came to get me, and as we drove back to my childhood home I struggled to process what had just happened. Why had I been spared the same outcome experienced by the other driver, who I was later told had a long recovery ahead of her? Why was my head-on collision result so minor? It didn't take very long to conclude that I had just experienced a real-life miracle.

Days after the accident, I couldn't seem to shake the uneasiness of my newfound circumstances. To make matters worse, I continued to replay the moment of impact over and over in my head, rather than being thankful I had survived and wasn't six feet under. I focused on the negative, and for a moment I found myself trying to drag other people into my misery.

Thankfully, just like the sit-for-a-bit lady, I was about to receive another important piece of wisdom—from my mom and dad.

It was early in the morning and my whiplash had now fully arrived. Downstairs, I heard my father holler at my mom, "Nanny, can you put my socks on please?" It was all I could do to get out of my bed, but I decided I would try anyway. Needless to say, that didn't go well. I ended up starting my day facedown on the floor, buck naked.

Struggling to get up, I suddenly had a moment of fear, realizing that my mom might come up to see what had caused the *thud* on the floor. I ungracefully rolled from side to side until I was able to slip my underwear on.

Let's just say I've had better moments.

After I found my way back to my feet, I hobbled downstairs to join Dad in his daily world of requiring help to get dressed because of a stroke he'd suffered, and the debilitating effects from having contracted West Nile virus.

As I sat beside him, Mom finished pulling his socks on. She then lovingly looked at me and said, "I'll help you next."

This would have been such a wonderful opportunity to be thankful. Instead I selfishly blurted out, "I hate not being able to dress myself. It's all I can do to put my own underwear on. This is brutal!"

Well, my unthankful comment went over like a lead balloon. In less than .054 seconds, I received a I-should-kick-your-behind stare from my dad.

"At least you have your mom helping you," he said. "I don't know what I would do without her."

To be honest, I was a little surprised at how quick and pointed his response was, but he was right. It's so easy to do something for others when you believe you'll get a reward, but being thankful for what you have is a choice! My mom stood to gain nothing from helping us get dressed, and yet she did it anyway. In fact, she has been blessing our family with her kind and loving spirit for as long as I can remember.

In the past, I often felt bad for her, because she never put herself first. She asked for nothing. Looking back, I now realize that she went without so that we all got what we wanted. Then, in her golden years of her life, my father became disabled due to several medical conditions and thus he slowly but surely became her full-time occupation. She could have complained endlessly or simply packed up and left for greener pastures, but she never did. Instead she loved on him like she had promised to do so some fifty odd years earlier.

She has always given back and continues to help out our entire family in any way she can. Why? Because that's where her joy and happiness comes from, not from stuff! To say my mom is a model of thankfulness would be an understatement.

I would like to close off the book with an excerpt from a conversation Mom and I had from a time in her life when my father had become fully dependent on her.

"Mom, you do so much for everybody," I said. "Why don't you get respite for Dad so you can enjoy some time for yourself? You deserve that."

"Derek, what I do for your dad is not a chore," she replied selflessly. "I don't mind doing it. He would do it for me. That's what life is all about. I know he's thankful for it and that's all that matters. Plus, who would be crazy enough to take care of that old bugger and his antics anyway?"

If my mom's approach to life isn't the essence of thankfulness, I don't know what is. I hope her actions and words inspire you to want to do the same. Thanks for the teaching, **Mom. Without a doubt, you are the best mom ever!**

Be cheerful no matter what; pray all the time;
thank God no matter what happens.
This is the way God wants you
who belong to Christ Jesus to live.
(1 Thesslonians 5:16-18, emphasis added)

Appendix
Janice's Blog Post

The following is a blog post that links back to Janice's story in Chapter Fourteen. Janice referenced it in our interview, and I would be remiss if I didn't include it. It in itself presents such a great teaching.

My decision to go on antidepressants wasn't one I came to easily. I tried everything I could think of to avoid it. I've tried a lot of natural health things that helped and a lot that didn't. I'm not here to try to sell you on the one silver bullet that fixed all my problems. I haven't found one of those yet, but what I have found is that change comes one little step at a time. I know, it's not sexy, but lasting change is more about the little daily decisions we make and an effort to keep improving. For me, meds were a piece of that puzzle, along with a functional medicine approach, exercise and a healthy spiritual life. Could the discovery of some diet plan, supplement regiment, Bible study, gratitude journal or psychotherapy replace my need for meds? Maybe. I'm not done my search yet, so I'll let you know. But in the meantime, I'm going to LIVE MY LIFE, which is something I really wasn't doing before I made the decision to get some help. I came across a journal entry I made many years ago. It is titled, "Why I'm going on meds":

Not because prayer doesn't work.

Not because my life is so bad or I can't control my thoughts.

Not because God has abandoned me in that area and I'm on my own.

Not because I'm down every day. Or I want to hurt myself or others.

But because...

I want to BUILD instead of just SURVIVE.

I want to build confidence, not just maintain with a three steps ahead and two back pattern.

I want to build new relationships, not retreat.

I want to build a closer relationship with God, my family, new friends; not only a couple weeks a month, but every day.

I want to build new habits of dealing with stress and my emotions—in a healthier way.

I want more patience, affection and words of affirmation to flow to my loved ones.

I want to be able to RECEIVE God's unconditional love and the love of others.

I want to stop thinking about me so much and start to really fulfil my purpose effectively.

I want to form new habits that I can be proud to model to my kids. No more being critical and judgmental of myself or them. After all, if I'm spending all my energy on trying to just maintain an "okay" thought life, what energy is left to pour out to others? I'm ready to feel good about my life.

www.ingramcontent.com/pod-product-compliance
Lightning Source LLC
Chambersburg PA
CBHW021145090426
42740CB00008B/956

* 9 7 8 1 4 8 6 6 2 1 1 7 0 *